Poems From The Little Flower Of Jesus

by
Saint Teresa of Lisieux

Translated by
Susan L. Emery

"Thou, O Lord, hast been the only object of my songs in the place of my pilgrimage."
Ps. CXVIII, 54.

St Athanasius Press
All Rights Reserved 2018

ISBN-13: 978-1727557206

ISBN-10: 1727557204

St Athanasius Press
melwaller@gmail.com
(email is the best way to reach us)
www.stathanasiuspress.com

Specializing in Reprinting Catholic Classics

CONTENTS

Introduction	5
First Part	
My Song Of Today	10
To Live Of Love	10
Canticle To The Holy Face	14
Thou Hast Broken My Bonds, O Lord	15
Remember Thou	16
To The Sacred Heart.	25
The Eternal Canticle Sung In Banishment	26
"I Thirst For Love"	28
My Heaven On Earth.	30
My Hope	31
My Wishes Before The Tabernacle.	32
Jesus Only	34
To Scatter Flowers	35
A Work Of Love	36
My Armor	37
My Peace And My Joy	39
A Lily Amidst Thorns	41
A Withered Rose	42
Abandonment	43
Second Part	
The Dew Divine	46
To Our Lady Of Victories	47
The Queen Of Heaven To Her Little Mary	49
Why I Love Thee, Mary	51

Third Part

To My Angel Guardian	58
To My Little Brothers In Heaven, The Holy Innocents	59
Melody Of Saint Cecilia	62
Canticle Of Saint Agnes	65
To The Venerable Theophane Venard, Martyred	66

Fourth Part

Story Of A Sheperdess Who Became A Queen	69
Prayer Of The Child Of A Saint	71
What I Used To Love	74

Fifth Part

Jesus At Bethany	83
The Bird Cage Of The Infant Jesus	90
Flight Into Egypt	92
The Little Divine Beggar Of Christmas	95
Angels Of The Crib	106
Poems In Honor Of Jeanne D'Arc	115
Sheperdess Of Domremy Hearkening To Her Voices	115
Hymn Of Jeanne D'Arc After Her Victories	121
Prayer Of Jeanne D'Arc In Prison	122
Voices Of Jeanne D'Arc During Her Martyrdom	123
The Divine Judgment	124
Canticle Of Triumph	125
Prayer Of France To The Venerable Jeanne D'Arc	126
Canticle To Obtain Canonization Of Jeanne D'Arc	127

Introduction

MARIE FRANCOISE-THERESE MARTIN, daughter of Louis-Joseph-Stanislaus and Zelie (Guerin) Martin, was born in Alencon, France, January 2, 1873. She was the youngest of nine children, four of whom died in infancy, and of the five others, four became Carmelite nuns. Therese, a singularly precocious, charming and beautiful child set her heart upon entering the convent at the age of fifteen. Her wish was granted nearly to the letter, or on April 9, 1888, when only a little more than three months past her fifteenth birthday, she was received into the Carmelite monastery of the Sacred Heart of Jesus and of the Immaculate Conception, at Lisieux, France. There she lived for nine years a life of remarkably joyous and childlike or angelic holiness and there September 30, 1897, she died. Her name in religion was Sister Teresa of the Child Jesus and of the Holy Face. In her character she so exemplified the loveliness and the sanctity of the Child Jesus Himself, and to such a singular degree throughout her whole short life did she love and serve her Lord, that the Mother Prioress bade her write her memories, which, with entire openness and simple obedience, she did. After her death this exquisite memoir, at first intended only for the edification of her sister nuns, was published in French, together with a valuable appendix of her letters, notes of retreat, counsels, and certain loving remembrances of her life by those who had watched her daily. Following upon these, come one hundred and fifty pages that contain her poems, which she wrote in many instances to certain French airs. It has been said of these simple verses that: "The rules of prosody are not always exactly observed in their construction; and that on the other hand, they suggest an extraordinary degree of inspiration." Lifted up by an angelic presence, the soul shakes off the dust of earth, and rises gently towards the true ideal God, the eternal Love. In reading this charming history, containing verses that breathe exquisite purity, we fancy ourselves before a fresco of Fra Angelico; or, to use a graceful expression of Soeur Therese herself, we imagine that we hear a "melody from heaven."

It is a curious fact that Sister Teresa seems never to have written verses outside the cloister; though within its walls she succeeded, and to an extent by no means slight. She narrates her experience as follows to the prioress:

"O my Mother! How many reasons I have for thanking God! I am going to tell you in all simplicity, that the Lord showed to me the same mercy as to King Solomon. All my wishes have been fulfilled not only my wishes for perfection, but even those, the vanity of which I understood without having experienced it. Seeing one of my sisters paint charming pictures and compose verses, I thought how happy I should be if I could paint also, could express my thoughts in verse, and could do much good to others. Yet I would not have liked to ask for these natural gifts, and my wishes remained hidden in the depths of my heart. But Jesus, hidden likewise in that poor little heart, deigned to show it once more the nothingness of what passes away. To the great surprise of the community I composed poetry, I painted; it was permitted me to do good to some souls. And even as Solomon (Ecclesiastes 2: 11), turning himself to all the works which his hands had wrought, and to the labors wherein he had labored in vain, saw in all things vanity and vexation of mind, and that nothing was lasting under the sun, so I saw by experience, that the only joy on earth consists in hiding one's self, in remaining in complete ignorance of all created things. I understood that without love all works are but nothingness, even the most brilliant. Instead of doing me harm, and wounding my soul, the gifts the Lord lavished on me led me to Him. I perceive that He is the only thing that cannot change, the only thing capable of satisfying my immense desires."

One turns from these simple and holy songs with a conviction which is well expressed by P. N., "To the reader" in the beginning of the French edition of the Memoirs and which I have translated thus:

Would you live, one happy moment,
lifted between earth and heaven;
Feel an atmosphere supernal
all about you gently rise;
See the world beneath your feet and
walk 'mid radiant Pleiads seven;
And believe an angel walks beside you,
from more radiant skies ?
Read these songs of love with reverence;
let no idle glance profane
These sublimely simple pages,
seek their mystic sense to know;
But learn humbly that in convents
Love Divine as King doth reign,
And, within their deep seclusion,
hearts with joy are all aglow.
Lovely flower, soul celestial!
fifteen years at home you grew;

Then you gave your heart to Jesus,
fresh with its baptismal dew;
And the Sovereign Pontiff blessed this
lovely lily, that we know
As a nun whose wondrous sweetness,
heavenly, angelic ways,
Lyric songs of rapturous music,--
everything about her -- says
That an angel passed through Carmel,
just a few short years ago.

One remarkable thing about Sister Teresa's simple and sweet verses is the mortification she practiced in regard to them, a severe self-discipline which those will appreciate, who have tried to keep in mind thoughts which they could not at once write down. To quote her own words: "The good God never let our Mother tell me how to write my verses as fast as I composed them, and I would not have been willing to ask this permission for fear of committing a fault against holy poverty. So I waited for the hour of free time, and it was not without extreme difficulty, that I recalled at eight o'clock in the evening what I had composed in the morning. These little nothings are a martyrdom, it is true; but we must take great care not to make our martyrdom less meritorious, by allowing ourselves a thousand things that would make our religious life an easy one." Her verses have for their motto: "Vous avez été seul l'objet de mes chants dans le lieu de mon pélerinage," ("You alone are the object of my song in the place of my pilgrimage"), and are divided into five sections. The first consists of hymns and canticles relating more exclusively to her Lord, the Divine Spouse of her soul; the second part contains hymns in relation to the Blessed Virgin; and the remaining sections contain other hymns and poems and pious recreations, in honor of St. Mary Magdelen, St. Agnes, and St. Cecelia.

The religious spirit of the French people is surely not wholly dead if we may judge them from the fact, that twenty-nine thousand copies of the life a young Carmelite nun of Lisieux have been sold in that land, within a few years. A translation under the title of The Little Flower of Jesus, is known in English, but the entire French life appears in two forms: one, a large edition with the poems of the gifted young soul; the other without the poems except one under the title--which also forms the title of that edition--Une Rose Effeuillée.

Moreover, the life has been translated into Polish, German, Dutch, Italian and Portuguese. The Spanish and Flemis editions are nearing completion. The Cardinal Patriarch of Lisbon has granted an indulgence to those who read "this admirable Life," and all the Prelates of Portugal have followed his example. Truly the last desires of Sister Teresa have been realized in a touching and most wonderful manner: "I wish to pass my Heaven in doing good on earth," and again, "After my death I will let fall a shower of roses."

The Carmelites of Lisieux receive from all parts of the world, most precious testimonies of the truth of these words. At one time it is the account of the remarkale cure of some pitiful malady; more frequently it is to tell of the relief and consolation of a soul in distress. Persons come from long distances and foreign lands to kneel at the tomb of this elect of God. Priests and young missionaries departing for the Foreign Missions respectfully kiss the blessed earth and carry away flowers as veritable relics. The Nuns are constantly pressed to give some souvenir of the "little queen," "the little St. Teresa," the "little great Saint" or "the Little Flower", for so are her titles varied by the devotion of those who love her, the world over.

The Seminaries have addressed touching petitions covered with signatures earnestly pleading for the introduction of her Cause. Venerable Priests and eminent Religious have said:--

"Sister Teresa of the Infant Jesus is a providential soul. Her divine mission is evident."

"This dear 'little saint' is a remarkable Missionary whose word is powerful and irresistible."

"The Life of this soul written by herself has a lasting charm, and souls who yield to its powerful influence will be drawn from tepidity and sin."

"I assure you that the Lord works beautiful and great things by means of your 'little Saint.' In our Seminary she transforms souls."

"The heart of Sister Teresa is a pure flame of Paradise which has enkindled and will enkindled many hearts."

"Happy Victim, not only consumed by the flame of Divine Love but who has received the gift of communicating it powerfully to others."

"Many lives tell of the fire of Love. The Life of Sister Teresa makes it felt. Many give us the desire to love God; she puts the fire in our souls." O Thou who hast so loved Jesus and souls, who didst say when dying, "I have given my God only love, and he will return my love."--thy word was a prophecy. Thousands of hearts to whom thou wast hitherto unknown, love and venerate thee now, and by their prayers and desires long to hasten the day when the Church will enshrine thy memory on Her Altars.

Meanwhile, dear Little Flower, console the heart of the Sovereign Pontiff in this moment of supreme trial, and from the gardens of Paradise let fall upon Him and each of His children thy shower of roses.

First Part

MY SONG OF TO-DAY.

Oh! how I love Thee, Jesus! my soul aspires to Thee--
And yet for one day only my simple prayer I pray!
Come reign within my heart, smile tenderly on me,
        To-day, dear Lord, to-day.

But if I dare take thought of what the morrow brings--
That fills my fickle heart with dreary, dull dismay;
I crave, indeed, my God, trials and sufferings,
        But only for to-day!

O sweetest Star of heaven! O Virgin, spotless, blest,
Shining with Jesus' light, guiding to Him my way!
O Mother! 'neath thy veil let my tired spirit rest,
        For this brief passing day!

Soon shall I fly afar among the holy choirs,
Then shall be mine the joy that never knows decay;
And then my lips shall sing, to heaven's angelic lyres,
        The eternal, glad To-day!

    June, 1894.

TO LIVE OF LOVE

"If any man love Me, he will keep My word and
My Father will love him and We will come
to him and make Our abode with him.
My peace I give unto you. Abide
in My love."
(St. John 14, 23,27,-15:9)

The eve His life of love drew near its end,
Thus Jesus spoke: "Whoever loveth Me,
And keeps My word as Mine own faithful friend,
My Father, then and I his guests will be;

Within his heart will make Our dwelling above.
Our palace home, true type of heaven above.
There, filled with peace, We will that he shall rest,
    With us, in love.

Incarnate Word! Thou Word of God alone!
To live of love, 'tis to abide with Thee.
Thou knowest I love Thee, Jesus Christ, my Own!
Thy Spirit's fire of love enkindleth me.
By loving Thee, I draw the Father here
Down to my heart, to stay with me always.
Blest Trinity! Thou art my prisoner dear,
    Of love, to-day.

To live of love, 'tis by Thy life to live,
O glorious King, my chosen, sole Delight!
Hid in the Host, how often Thou dost give
Thyself to those who seek Thy radiant light.
Then hid shall be my life, unmarked, unknown,
That I may have Thee heart to heart with me;
For loving souls desire to be alone,
    With love, and Thee!

To live of love, 'tis not to fix one's tent
On Tabor's height and there with Thee remain.
'Tis to climb Calvary with strength nigh spent,
And count Thy heavy cross our truest gain.
In heaven, my life a life of joy shall be,
The heavy cross shall then be gone for aye.
Here upon earth, in suffering with Thee,
    Love! let me stay.

To live of love, 'tis without stint to give,
An never count the cost, nor ask reward;
So, counting not the cost, I long to live
And show my dauntless love for Thee, dear Lord!
O Heart Divine, o'erflowing with tenderness,
How swift I run, who all to Thee has given!
Naught but Thy love I need, my life to bless.
    That love is heaven!

To live of love, it is to know no fear;
No memory of past faults can I recall;
No imprint of my sins remaineth here;
The fire of Love divine effaces all.
O sacred flames! O furnace of delight!
I sing my safe sweet happiness to prove.
In these mild fires I dwell by day, by night.
        I live of love!

To live of love, 'tis in my heart to guard
A mighty treasure in a fragile vase.
Weak, weak, am I, O well-beloved Lord!
Nor have I yet an angel's perfect grace.
But, if I fall each hour that hurries by,
Thou com'st to me from Thy bright home above,
And, raising me, dost give me strength to cry:
        I live of love!

To live of love it is to sail afar
And bring both peace and joy where'er I be.
O Pilot blest! love is my guiding star;
In every soul I meet, Thyself I see.
Safe sail I on, through wind or rain or ice;
Love urges me, love conquers every gale.
High on my mast behold is my device:
        "By love I sail!"

To live of love, it is when Jesus sleeps
To sleep near Him, though stormy waves beat nigh.
Deem not I shall awake Him! On these deeps
Peace reigns, like that the Blessed know.on high.
To Hope, the vovage seems one little day;
Faith's hand shall soon the veil between remove;
'Tis Charity that swells my sail alway.
        I live of love!

To live of love, O Master dearest, best!
It is to beg Thee light Thy holiest fires
Within the soul of each anointed priest,
Till he shall feel the Seraphim's desires;

It is to beg Thee guard Thy Church, O Christ!
For this I plead with Thee by night, by day;
And give myself, in sacrifice unpriced,
        With love alway!

To live of love, it is to dry Thy tears,
To seek for pardon for each sinful soul,
To strive to save all men from doubts and fears,
And bring them home to Thy benign control.
Comes to my ear sin's wild and blasphemous roar;
So, to efface each day, that burning shame,
I cry: " O Jesus Christ! I Thee adore.
        I love Thy Name!"

To live of love, 'tis Mary's part to share,
To bathe with tears and odorous perfume
Thy holy feet, to wipe them with my hair,
To kiss them; then still loftier lot assume,
To rise, and by Thy side to take my place,
And pour my ointments on Thy holy head.
But with no balsams I embalm Thy Face!
        'Tis love, instead!

"To live of love, what foolishness she sings!"
So cries the world. "Renounce such idle joy!
Waste not thy perfumes on such trivial things.
In useful arts thy talents now employ!"
To love Thee, Jesus! Ah, this loss is gain;
For all my perfumes no reward seek I.
Quitting the world, I sing in death's sweet pain:
        Of love I die!

To die of love, O martyrdom most blest!
For this I long, this is my heart's desire;
My exile ends; I soon will be at rest.
Ye Cherubim, lend, lend to me your lyre!
O dart of Seraphim, O flame of love,
Consume me wholly; hear my ardent cry!
Jesu, make reall my dream! Come Holy Dove!
        Of love I die!

To die of love, behold my life's long hope!
God is my one exceeding great reward.
He of my wishes forms the end and scope;
Him only do I seek; my dearest Lord.
With passionate love for Him my heart is riven.
O may He quickly come! He draweth nigh!
Behold my destiny, behold my heaven,--
      OF LOVE TO DIE.

    February 25,1895

CANTICLE TO THE HOLY FACE.

Dear Jesus! 'tis Thy Holy Face
Is here the start that guides my way;
They countenance, so full of grace,
Is heaven on earth, for me, to-day.
And love finds holy charms for me
In Thy sweet eyes with tear-drops wet;
Through mine own tears I smile at Thee,
And in Thy griefs my pains forget.

How gladly would I live unknown,
Thus to console Thy aching heart.
Thy veiled beauty, it is shown
To those who live from earth apart.
I long to fly to Thee alone!

Thy Face is now my fatherland,--
The radiant sunshine of my days,--
My realm of love, my sunlit land,
Where, all life long, I sing Thy praise;
It is the lily of the vale,
Whose mystic perfume, freely given,
Brings comfort, when I faint and fail,
And makes me taste the peace of heaven.

Thy face, in its unearthly grace,
Is like the divinest myrrh to me,
That on my heart I gladly place;

It is my lyre of melody;
My rest -- my comfort-- is Thy Face.

My only wealth, Lord! is thy Face;
I ask naught else than this from Thee; Hid in the secret of that Face,
The more I shall resemble Thee!
Oh, leave on me some impress faint
Of Thy sweet, humble, patient Face,
And soon I shall become a saint,
And draw men to Thy saving grace.

So, in the secret of Thy Face,
Oh! hide me, hide me, Jesus blest!
Ther let me find its hidden grace,
Its holy fires, and, in heaven's rest,
Its rapturous kiss, in Thy embrace!
        August 12, 1895.

'THOU HAST BROKEN MY BONDS, O LORD'

(Psalm CXV.7.)
For a Postulant, on her entrance-day into Carmel.

Thou, Jesu! on this day my earthly bonds hast broken.
In Mary's Order old, my soul true goods shall find;
And if to-day: "farewell" my quivering lips have spoken
To those who loved me best, so dear, so true, so kind,
Thou, Lord, wilt be to them far more than I could be;
And Thou wilt deign to win some sinful souls through me.

Jesu! on Carmel I shall dwell--
Thy love has called Thy child to that oasis fair;
There I desire to serve Thee well,
To love Thee there, and then to die,
There! yes, my Jesu, there!

O Jesu! on this day, Thy loe my prayer has granted;
Before Thy altar throne hereafter 'tis my part
Calmly to wait for heaven,-- all pain to bear undaunted,--
And, lifting to the rays of Thy wihite Host my heart,

Within that fire of love all self to burn away,
And, like a seraph blest, to serve Thee night and day.

Ah, Jesu! 'twill be mine to dwell,
One day, with Thee on high, in heaven's bright
mansions fair
There evermore to love Thee well,
To love Thee, and no more to die,
There! yes, my Jesu, there!

    August 15, 1895.

JESUS, MY WELL BELOVED, REMEMBER THOU!

"My daughter, seek for those of My Words, that breathe forth the most love; write them, and then, guarding them with great care, as you would holy relics,
be sure that you read them often. When a friend desires to re-awaken in the heart of his friend the first freshness and warmth of his affection, he says to him : 'Do you remember your feelings when you said such a word to me one day?'
or again: 'Do you remember what you felt on such an occasion? in such a place?
at such a time?' In like manner do you, too, believe that the most precious relics of Me to be found on earth today are the words of My love, the words that came from the depths of My loving Heart."
Our Divine Lord to St. Gertrude.

Recall, O Christ! the Father's glories bright,
Recall the splendors of Thy heavenly home,
Which Thou didst leave, to come to earth's dark night,
And save poor sinners who in exile roam!
Dear Jesus! bending down at Mary's humble word,
In her Thou didst conceal Thy majesty adored.
Now that maternal breast,
Thy second heaven, Thy rest,
Remember Thou!

Remember, now, the day of Thy blest birth,
How angels, quitting heaven, sang joyously:
"To God be power, glory, lasting worth;
And peace to men of good will ever be!"
For nineteen hundred years Thy promise Thou hast kept;
Thy children in that peace have waked, and worked, and slept.
To taste forever here
Thy peace, divinely dear,
I seek Thee now.

Remember O Thou Babe in swaddling bands!
Beside Thy crib I would forever stay.
There, with Thine angels, Lord of all the lands!
I would remind thee of that happy day.
O Jesus! call to mind the shepherds and wise men,
Who offered Thee their hearts, as I mine own again;
The Babes of Bethlehem see,
Who gave their blood for Thee.
Remember Thou!

Remember Thou that Mary's holy arms
Thou didst prefer to any royal throne.
Dear little One! she shielded Thee from harm,
She fed Thee with her virginal milk alone.
Oh, at that feast of love Thy mother gave to Thee,
My little Brother, grant that I a guest may be,
Thy little sister I.
Oh, hear my ardent cry:
Remember Thou!

Remember that Thy childish voice, dear Lord!
Called Joseph father, who, at heaven's decree,
Prevailed to snatch Thee from the tyrant's sword,
And sought old Egypt's far off coast with Thee.
O Word of God! recall what mysteries round Thee woke;
Thou didst keep silent, Lord! the while an angel spoke.
Thy distant, long exile
On banks of ancient Nile,
Remember now.

Remember Thou that on my native shore,
The stars of gold, the moon of silver bright,
Which I contemplate, wondering more and more,
Charmed in the East Thine infant eyes at night.
That tiny hand of Thine, that stroked Thy Mother's face,
Sustained the world, held all things in their place;
And Thou didst think of me!
Ah! how I think of Thee,
Remember now.

Remember Thou, in solitude most blest,
Thou laboredst with Thy hands for daily bread.
To live forgotten,-- this Thy earnest quest,
All human wisdom trampled 'neath Thy tread,
One single word of Thine could charm a listening world;
Yet Thou Thy wisdom kept in closest silence furled.
Thou, Who didst all things know,
No sign of power wouldst show.
Remember Thou!

Remember how, - Stranger and Pilgrim here,
Thou hadst no'home, O Thou Eternal Word!
Not e'en a pillow for Thy head most dear;
Not e'en a shelter, like the flitting bird.
O Jesu, come to me! Rest Thou upon my breast.
Come, Come! My spirit longs to have Thee for its Guest.
Thou well beloved, adored!
Rest in my heart, dear Lord,
Ever as now!

Remember Thou, the loving tenderness
That Thou didst show to children seeking Thee.
Like them I would receive Thy kind caress;
Like them, Thy blessings, Lord, be granted me.
That I in heaven may gain Thy welcome and Thy rest,
Here will I practise well all childhood's virtues best.
"The childlike soul wins heaven."
This promise Thou hast given,
Remember Thou!
Remember Thou that on the fountain's brink,-

A traveller, weary with the journey's length,-
Thou of the sinful tenderly didst think,
And for contrition gave her lasting strength.
I know Thee well Who asked, of her, the draught, that day.
Thou art "the Gift of God," the Life, the Truth the Way.
Thou wilt not pass me by.
I hear Thy tender cry:
"Come to Me now!"

"Come unto Me, poor souls with sorrow tost!
Your heavy load My hands shall take away;
Your griefs and pains shall be forever lost,
Within the depths of love I feel for aye."
I thirst, I thirst, O Christ! Nought else I seek, save Thee.
Borne down beneath my cross, I cry: "O comfort me!"
Be Thy dear love my home!
I come! Yes, Lord, I come!
Receive me now!

Remember Thou that, though a child of light,
Too oft, alas! I have neglected Thee.
Take pity on me in life's dreary night;
Oh, pardon all my sin and misery!
Make my sad heart rejoice Thy holy will to do;
My soul to those delights, hid in Thy gospels, woo!
That I that book of gold
Ever most dear did hold,
Remember Thou!

Remember Thou Thy holy Mother's power
That she possesses o'er Thy Heart divine.
Remember, at her prayer, one joyful hour,
Thou didst change water to delicious wine.
Deign also to transform my works, though poor they be;
Oh, make them glorious works, when Mary pleads with Thee.
That I am Mary's child,
Dear Jesus, meek and mild,
Remember Thou!

Remember that the summits of the hills
Thou often didst ascend at set of sun.
Ah! how Thy prayer the long, long night hours fills,
Thy chants of praise when weary day is done.
Thy prayer I offer now, with ever new delight,
Joined to my own poor prayers, my office, day and night.
That I, too, near Thy heart,
Take in Thy prayer my part,
Remember Thou!

Remember that Thine eyes beheld the fields
White to the harvest,- harvest of the blest!
Thy Heart o'er them Its mystic influence wields;
Within that Heart is room for all, and rest.
That soon may come for Thee Thy glorious harvest day,
I immolate myself, I offer prayers alway.
I give my joys, my tears,
For thy good harvesters.
Remember Thou!

Recall that feast of angels in delight,
That harmony of heaven's kingly host,
The joy of all those choirs of spirits bright,
When one is saved, once counted 'mongst the lost.
Oh, how I would augment that joy and glory there!
For sinners I will pray with ceaseless, ardent prayer.
To win dear souls to heaven,
My life and prayers are given.
Remember Thou!

Remember that most holy flame of love
Thou wouldst enkindle in all hearts alway.
To me it came from Thy fair heaven above;
Would I could spread its fires by night and day!
One feeble spark, dear Lord!- O glorious mystery!-
A fire immense can light, if fanned to flame by Thee.
I long, Divinest Star!
To bear Thy flames afar.
Remember Thou!

Remember how the festal board was graced,
To feast the penitent returning son!
Remember, too, the innocent soul is placed
Ever near Thee, O Thou Beloved One!
Unto the prodigal no welcome is denied;
But, ah! the elder son is always at Thy side.
Father, and Love Divine,
All that Thou hast is mine.
Remember Thou!

Remember how Thou didst disdain earth's pride,
When working miracles with God's own ease.
"Ye who seek human praise! can ye decide
To give your faith to mysteries like these?
The great works that I do, (so Thou hast said, dear Lord!)
My friends shall yet surpass, according to My word."
How humble Thou wast then,
Among the sons of men.
Remember Thou!

Remember in what rapture of delight
The loved apostle rested on Thy Heart.
In that deep peace he knew Thy love and might;
Thy mysteries thence he drew, - how strong Thou art!
Of Thy beloved John I feel no jealousy.
I am Thy choice; I, too, behold the mystery.
I, too, upon Thy breast
May have ecstatic rest.
Remember Thou!

Recall Thine awful hour of agony
When blood and tears bore witness to Thy woe.
O pearls of love! O rubies fair to see!
Thence virginal blooms of beauty ever grow.
An angel, showing Thee what harvest Thou shouldst reap,
Gave gladness to Thee, then, even while Thou didst weep.
Then truly didst Thou see,
Amongst those lilies, me!
Remember now!

Thy blood, Thy tears, - a fruitful living source,
Those mystic flowers, makes virginal evermore;
And to them grants a wondrous, holy force,
For winning souls to serve Thee and adore.
A virginal heart is mine; yet, Christ, what mystery!
Mother of souls am I, through my chaste bond with Thee.
These virginal flowers that bloom
To bring poor sinners home,
Remember Thou!

Remember Thou, that, steeped in direst woe,
Condemned by men, to heaven Thine eyes were raised;
And Thou didst cry: " Soon ye My power shall know.
Soon shall ye hear My name by angels praised! "
Yet who believed Thee, then, the Son of God to be,
Thy glory veiled and hid in our humanity?
Fairest of sons of men!
My God! I knew Thee then!
Remember now!

Remember that Thy dear, divinest Face,
Even among Thy friends, was oft unknown.
But Thou hast drawn me by its matchless grace;
Thou knowest well I claimed it for mine own.
I have divined its charms, tho' wet with human tears.
Face of Eternal God! I love Thee all these years.
Part of my name Thou art!
Thou dost console my heart.
Remember Thou! *

Remember Thou that amorous complaint,
Escaping from Thy lips on Calvary's tree:
"I thirst!" Oh, how my heart like Thine doth faint.
Yes, yes! I share Thy burning thirst with Thee.
The more my heart burns bright with Thy great Heart's chaste fires,
The more I thirst for souls, to quench Thy Heart's desires.
That with such love always
I burn, by night, by day,
Remember Thou!

Remember, O my Jesu! Word of life!
That Thou hast loved me, dying e'en for me.
Oh, let me be with holy folly rife!
So would I, also, live and die for Thee!
Thou knowest, Lord! my wish, my loving heart's desire, -
To make Thee loved, and then, in martyrdom expire.
I long of love to die.
O hear my ardent cry.
Remember Thou!

Recall that glorious, that victorious hour,
When Thou didst say: "Happy indeed is he,
Who has not seen My triumph and My power,
But, seeing not, has still believed in Me."
In faith's dim, shadowy night, I love Thee, I adore.
Jesu, I wait in peace, till faith's long night is o'er.
That not one wish had I
To see Thee 'neath this sky,
Remember Thou!

Remember that ascending unto God,
Thou wouldst not leave us orphans sad and lone,
But didst, a Prisoner still, where we abode,
Veil on our altars all Thy pomp, my Own!
The shadow of Thy veil is, oh! how pure and bright,
Thou Living Bread of faith, heaven's Food, my heart's Delight.
O mystery of love!
My Bread from heaven above,
Jesus, 'tis Thou!

Remember Thou, in spite of insults hurled
Against this sacrament of love divine,
Thou dost remain in this dull, weary world,
And fix Thy dwelling in a heart like mine.
O Bread of exiled souls! holy and heavenly Host!
No more I live -not I! in Thee my life is lost.
Thy chosen ciborium
Am I. Come, Jesu, come!
My Love art Thou.

Thy sanctuary here, dear Lord, am I,
That evil men shall never dare molest.
Rest in my, heart! Oh, do not pass me by!
Thy garden I, each flower an offering blest.
But if from me Thou turn, white Lily of the vale!
I know too well those flowers would wither and would fail.
Ever, Thou Lily rare!
Bloom in my garden fair.
My life art Thou!

Remember that I longed upon this earth,
To comfort Thee for sinners' scorn of Thee.
Give me a thousand hearts to praise Thy worth.
My Well Beloved! abide, abide with me!
A thousand hearts too few would be for my desire;
Give me Thy Heart to set my longing heart on fire.
My ardent love for Thee,
While swift the moments flee,
Remember Thou!
Remember, Lord! that Thy dear will alone
Is my sole wish, my only happiness.
I give myself to Thee, to rest, mine Own!
With Thee in peace, and know Thy power to bless.
And if Thou seems't to sleep while raging waves beat high,
In peace I still remain, without one anguished cry.
In peace, on Thee, I wait;
But, for th' Awakening great,
Prepare me Thou!

Remember how I often long and sigh
For that last day when angels shall proclaim:
"Time is no more! The judgment draweth nigh.
Rise thou, to face thy judge! He calls thy name."
Then swiftly shall I fly, past bounds of earth in space,
To live at last within the Vision of Thy Face.
That it alone can be
My joy eternally,
Remember Thou!

        October 21, 1895.

TO THE SACRED HEART

Beside the tomb wept Magdalen at dawn,-
She sought to find the dead and buried Christ;
Nothing could fill the void now He was gone,
No one to soothe her burning grief sufficed.
Not even you, Archangels heaven assigned!
To her could bring content that dreary day.
Your buried King, alone, she longed to find,
And bear His lifeless body far away.

Beside His tomb she there the last remained,
And there again was she before the sun;
There, too, to come to her the Saviour deigned,-
He would not be, by her, in love outdone.
Gently He showed her then His bless~d Face,
And one word sprang from His deep Heart's recess:
Maryl His voice she knew, she knew its grace;
It came with perfect peace her heart to bless.

One day, my God! I, too, like Magdalen,
Desired to find Thee, to draw near to Thee;
So, over earth's immense, stretching plain,
I sought its Master and its King to see
. Then cried I, though I saw the flowers bloom
In beauty 'neath green trees and azure skies:
O brilliant Naturel thou art one vast tomb,
Unless God's Face shall greet my longing eyes."
A heart I need, to soothe me and to bless,-
A strong support that can not pass away,-
To love me wholly, e'en my feebleness,
And never leave me through the night or day.
There is not one created thing below,
Can love me truly, and can never die.
God become man none else' my needs can know;
He, He alone, can understand my cry.

Thou comprehendest all I need, dear Lord!
To win my heart, from heaven Thou didst come;
For me Thy blood didst shed, O King adored!

And on our altars makest Thy home.
So, if I may not here behold Thy Face,
Or catch the heaenly music of Thy Voice,
I still can live, each moment, by Thy grace,
And in Thy Sacred Heart I can rejoice.

O Heart of Jesus, wealth of tenderness!
My joy Thou art, in Thee I safely hide.
Thou, Who my earliest youth didst charm and bless,
Till my last evening, oh! with me abide,
All that I had, to Thee I wholly gave,
To Thee each deep desire of mine is known.
Whoso his life shall lose, that life shall save;-
Let mine be ever lost in Thine alone!

I know it well, -no righteousness of mine
Hath any value in Thy searching eyes;
Its every breath my heart must draw from Thine,
To make of worth my life's long sacrifice.
Thou hast not found Thine angels without taint;
Thy Law amid the thunderbolts was given;
And yet, my Jesus! I nor fear nor faint.
For me, on Calvary, Thy Heart was riven.
To see Thee in Thy glory face to face,-
I know it well, - the soul must pass through fires.
Choose I on earth my purgatorial place, -
The flaming love of Thy great Heart's desires!
So shall my exiled soul, to death's command,
Make answer with one cry of perfect love;
Then flying straight to heaven its Fatherland,
Shall reach with no delay that home above.

    October, 1895.

THE ETERNAL CANTICLE.
SUNG IN BANISHMENT.

Exiled afar from heaven, I still, dear Lord, can sing, -
I, Thy betrothed, can sing the eternal hymn of love;
For, spite of exile comes to me, on dove like wing,

Thy Holy Spirit's fire of rapture from above.
Beauty supreme! my Love Thou art;
Thyself Thou givest all to me.
Oh, take my heart, my yearning heart, -
Make of my life one act of love to Thee!

Canst Thou my worthlessness efface?
In heart like mine canst make Thy home?
Yes, love wins love,-O wondrous grace!
I love Thee, love Thee! Jesu, come I
Love that enkindleth me,
Pierce and inflame me;
Come, for I cry to Thee!
Come and be mine
! Thy love it urgeth me;
Fain would I ever be
Sunken and lost in Thee,
Furnace divine!
All pain bome for Thee
Changes to joy for me,
When my love flies to Thee,
Winged like the dove.
Heavenly Completeness,
Infinite Sweetness,
My soul possesseth Thee
Here, as above.
Heavenly Completeness,
Infinite sweetness,

Naught else art Thou but Love! *Note: The swiftly varying metres of this rapturous "Canticle" evidently are
meant to indicate the ever increasing ecstasy of the singer; unless, indeed, Soeur Theresa had no explicit intention, but was simply carried on by the force
of a quasi inspiration.

       March 19, 1896.

"I THIRST FOR LOVE."

In wondrous love Thou didst come down from heaven
To immolate Thyself, O Christ, for me;
So, in my turn, my love to Thee is given,
I wish to suffer and to die for Thee.

Thou, Lord, hast spoken this truth benign:
"To die for one loved tenderly
Of greatest love on earth is sign;"
And now, such love is mine,--
Such love for Thee!

Abide, abide with me, O Pilgrim blest!
Behind the hill fast sinks the dying day.
Helped by Thy cross I mount the rocky crest;
Oh, come, to guide me on my heavenward way.

To be like Thee is my desire;
Thy voice finds echo in my soul.
Suffering I crave! Thy words of fire
Lift me above earth's mire,
And sin's control.

Chanting Thy victories, gloriously sublime,
The Seraphim - all heaven - cry to me,
That even Thou, to conquer sin and crime,
Upon this earth a sufferer needs must be.

For me, upon life's dreary way,
What scorn, what anguish, Thou didst bear
Let me grow humble every day
, Be least of all, alway,
Thy lot to share!

Ah, Christ! Thy great example teaches me
Myself to humble, honors to despise.
Little and low like Thee I choose to be,
Forgetting self, so I may charm Thine eyes.
My peace I find in solitude,

Nor ask I more, dear Lord, than this:
Be Thou my sole beatitude,
Ever, in Thee, renewed
My joy, my bliss!

Thou, the great God Whom earth and heaven adore,
Thou dwellest a prisoner for me night and day;
And every hour I hear Thy voice implore:
" I thirst I thirst I thirst for love alway!

I, too, Thy prisoner am I;
I, too, cry ever unto Thee
Thine own divine and tender cry:
"I thirst! Oh, let me die
Of love for Thee!"

For love of Thee I thirst! Fulfil my hope;
Augment in me Thine own celestial flame!
For love of Thee I thirst! Too scant earth's scope.
The glorious Vision of Thy Face I claim!

My long slow martyrdom of fire
Still more and more consumeth me.
Thou art my joy, my one desire.
Jesu! may I expire
Of love for Thee!

   April 30, 1806.

MY HEAVEN ON EARTH.

To bear my exile now, within this world of tears,
The holy tender glance of Christ, my Lord, I need.
That glance, surcharged with love, consoles me through the years;
His loveliness displays foretaste of heaven indeed.
On me my Jesus smiles, when toward Him I aspire,
The trial of my faith then weighs no more on me.
That love glance of my God, that smile of holy fire,
Oh, this is heaven for me!

'Tis heaven to have the power, great grace from Christ to win
For Holy Mother Church, for all my Sisters dear,-
For every soul on earth that He may enter in,
Enflame our sinful hearts, and grant us joy and cheer.
All things my love can gain when, heart to heart, I pray,
Alone with Jesus Christ in speechless ecstasy.
Beside His altar blest with Him I gladly stay,--
Oh, this is heaven for me!

My heaven within the Host safe hid and peaceful, lies,
Where Jesus Christ abides, divinest, fairest Fair.
From that great fount of love doth endless life arise;
There, day and night, my Lord doth hearken to my prayer.
When, in Thy perfect love (O moment blest and bright!)
Thou comest, Spouse most pure, me to transform in Thee,
That union of our hearts, that rapture of delight,-
Oh, this is heaven for me!

My heaven it is to feel in me some likeness blest
To Him Who made me and my soul hath reconciled;
My heaven it is always beneath His eye to rest.
To call Him Father dear, and be His loving child.
Safe shielded in His arms, no storm my soul can fear;
Complete abandonment my only law shall be.
To sleep upon His Heart, with His blest Face so near,-
Oh, this is heaven for me!

My heaven is God alone, the Trinity Divine,
Who dwells within my heart, the Prisoner of my love.

There, contemplating Thee, I tell Thee Thou art mine;
Thee will I love and serve until we meet above.
My heaven it is to smile on Thee whom I adore,
E'en when, to try my faith, from me Thou hidest Thee;
Calmly on Thee to smile, until Thou smil'st once more,-
Oh, this is heaven to me!
        June 7, 1896.

MY HOPE.

Though in a foreign land I dwell afar,
I taste in dreams the endless joys of heaven.
Fain would I fly beyond the farthest star,
And see the wonders to the ransomed given!
No more the sense of exile weighs on me,
When once I dream of that immortal day.
To my true fatherland, dear God! I see,
For the first time I soon shall fly away.

Ah! give me, Jesus! wings as white as snow,
That unto Thee I soon may take my flight.
I long to be where flowers unfading blow;
I long to see Thee, O my heart's Delight!
I long to fly to Mary's mother arms,-
To rest upon that spotless throne of bliss;
And, sheltered there from troubles and alarms,
For the first time to feel her gentle kiss.

Thy first sweet smile of welcoming delight
Soon show, O Jesus! to Thy lowly bride;
O'ercome with rapture at that wondrous sight,
Within Thy Sacred Heart, ah! let me hide.
O happy moment! and O heavenly grace!
When I shall hear Thee, Jesus, speak to me;
And the full vision of Thy glorious Face
For the first time my longing eyes shall see.

Thou knowest well, my only martyrdom
Is love, O Heart of Jesus Christ! for Thee;
And if my soul craves for its heavenly home,

'Tis but to love Thee more, eternally.
Above, when Thy sweet Face unveiled I view,
Measure nor bounds shall to my love be given;
Forever my delight shall seem as new
As the first time my spirit entered heaven.

    June 12, 1896.

MY WISHES BEFORE THE TABERNACLE.

O little key! I envy thee,
For thou canst ope, at any hour,
The Eucharistic prison house,
Where dwells the God of Love and Power.
And yet - Oh, tender mystery!-
One effort of my faith alone
Unlocks the tabernacle door,
And hides me there with Christ my Own.

O lamp within the holy place,
Whose mystic lights forever shine!
I fain would burn with fires of love
As bright, before my God and thine.
Yet, miracle of wondrous bliss!
Such flames are mine; and, day by day,
I can win souls to Jesus Christ,
To burn with His pure love for aye.
O consecrated altar stone!
I envy thee with every morn.
As once in Bethlehem's blessed shed,
The Eternal Word on thee is born.
Yet, gentle Saviour! hear my plea;
Enter my heart, O Lord divine!
'Tis no cold stone I offer Thee,
Who dost desire this heart of mine!

O corporal that angels guard!
What envy of thee fills my breast!
On thee, as in His swaddling bands,
I see my only Treasure rest.

Ah Virgin Mother! change my heart
Into a corporal pure and fair,
Whereon the snow white Host may rest,
And thy meek Lamb find shelter there.

O holy paten! Jesus makes
Of Thee His sacramental throne.
Ah! if He would abase Himself,
To dwell awhile with me alone!
Jesus fulfils my longing hope,
Nor must I wait until I die; -
He comes to me! He lives in me!
His ostensorium am I!

The chalice, too, I fain would be,
Where I adore the Blood divine!
Yet, at the holy sacrifice,
That Precious Blood each day is mine.
More dear to Jesus is my soul,
Than chalices of gold could be;
His altar is a Calvary new,
Whereon His Blood still flows for me.

Only one little bunch of grapes
That gladly disappears for Thee,
O Jesus, holy, heavenly Vine!
Thou knowest I rejoice to be.
Beneath the pressure of the cross,
I prove my love for Thee alway;
And ask no other joy than this,-
To immolate myself each day!

Among the grains of purest wheat,
O happy lot! he chooses me.
We lose our life for Him, the Christ,--
What rapturous height of ecstasy!
Thy spouse am I, Thy chosen one.
My Well Beloved! come, dwell in me.
Thy beauty wins my heart. Oh, come!
Deign to transform me into Thee!   1896.

JESUS ONLY

WRITTEN FOR A NOVICE.

Oh, how my heart would spend itself, to bless;
It hath such need to prove its tenderness!
And yet what heart can my heart comprehend?
What heart shall always love me without end?
All - all in vain for such return seek I;
Jesus alone my soul can satisfy.
Naught else contents or charms me here below;
Created things no lasting joy bestow.

My peace, my joy, my love, O Christ!
'Tis Thou alone! Thou hast sufficed.

Thou didst know how to make a mother's heart;
Tenderest of fathers, Lord! to me Thou art.
My only Love, Jesus, Divinest Word!
More than maternal is Thy heart, dear Lord!
Each moment Thou my way dost guard and guide;
I call - at once I find Thee at my side -
And if, sometimes Thou hid'st Thy face from me,
Thou com'st Thyself to help me seek for Thee.

Thee, Thee, alone I choose: I am Thy bride.
Unto Thy arms I hasten, there to hide.
Thee would I love, as little children love;
For Thee, like warrior bold, my love I'd prove.
Now, like to children, full of joy and glee,
So come I, Lord! to show my love to Thee;
Yet, like a warrior bold with high elation,
Rush I to combats in my blest vocation.

Thy Heart is Guardian of our innocence;
Not once shall it deceive my confidence.
Wholly my hopes are placed in Thee, dear Lord!
After long exile, I Thy Face adored
In heaven shall see. When clouds the skies o'erspread.
To Thee, my Jesus! I lift up my head;

For, in Thy tender glance, these words I see:
"O child! I made My radiant heaven for thee."

I know it well my burning tears and sighs
Are full of charm for Thy benignant eyes.
Strong seraphs form in heaven Thy court divine,
Yet Thou dost seek this poor weak heart of mine.
Ah! take my heart! Jesus, 'tis Thine alone;
All my desires I yield to Thee, my Own!
And all my friends, that are so loved by me,
No longer will I love them, save in Thee!

    August 15, 1896.

TO SCATTER FLOWERS.

O Jesu! O my Love! Each eve I come to fling
Before Thy sacred Cross sweet flowers of all the year.
By these plucked petals bright, my hands how gladly bring,
I long to dry Thine every tear!

To scatter flowers! - that means each sacrifice,
My lightest sighs and pains, my heaviest, saddest hours,
My hopes, my joys, my prayers, I will not count the price.
Behold my flowers!

With deep, untold delight Thy beauty fills my soul.
Would I might light this love in hearts of all who live!
For this, my fairest flowers, all things in my control,
How fondly, gladly I would give!
To scatter flowers! - behold my chosen sword
For saving sinners' souls and filling heaven's bowers.
The victory is mine: yes, I disarm Thee, Lord,
With these my flowers!

The petals in their flight caress Thy Holy Face;
They tell Thee that my heart is Thine, and Thine alone.
Thou knowest what these leaves are saying in my place;
On me Thou smilest from Thy throne.

To scatter flowers! - that means, to speak of Thee,--
My only pleasure here, where tears fill all the hours;
But soon, with angel hosts, my spirit shall be free,
To scatter flowers!

    June 28, 1896

A WORK OF LOVE.

A CANTICLE FOR THE SACRISTANS OF CARMEL, AND FOR THOSE SISTERS WHOSE OFFICE IT IS TO MAKE THE ALTAR BREADS.

What from our lot could us entice!
'Tis ours the altar breads to make
For that tremendous sacrifice
Where Christ is offered for our sake.

Heaven will be here, on sinful earth,
When hid beneath these veils of snow:
And God be here, in a new birth,
Come down to dwell with us below!

No queens are reigning anywhere
In joy as great as ours today
Our very work is love and prayer,
And binds our Spouse to us alway.
Earth's highest honors seem as naught,
Beside this service of Heaven's King;
Beside this peace, with blessings fraught
That Jesus sends on dove like wing.

A holy envy fills our hearts
For this fair work of our delight:
For these small snow white hosts, whose arts
Shall hide the Lamb of God from sight.
Yet we His brides, His chosen, are;
Our Friend is He, our Spouse is He!
And hosts are we, that He, our Star,
Transforms to light and ecstasy.

The priest's high lot is like our own,
In this our daily work for God.
Transformed by Him, we tread alone
The very path that He once trod.

By prayers, by acts of love divine,
His brave apostles we must aid;
With them our grace we must combine,
And fight their battles unafraid.

God, hid beneath these snowy veils,
Will hide Him, too, our hearts within.
O miracle! our prayer prevails,
With Him, for mercy upon sin.

Our joy, our glory, our delight,
O Jesus! is this work for Thee.
Thy Heaven is these ciboriums bright
Our prayers shall fill with souls for Thee.

       November, 1896.

MY ARMOR.

TO A NOVICE FOR HER PROFESSION DAY.

"The spouse of the King is terrible as an army set in array; She is like to a choir of music on a field of battle." Canticles vi. 3; vii.

"Put you on the armor of God that you may be able to stand against the deceits of the devil." Ephesians vi. II.

With heavenly armor am I clad today;
The hand of God has thus invested me.
What now from Him could tear my heart away;
What henceforth come between my God and me?
With Him for Guide, the fight I face serene;
Nor furious fire, nor foe, nor death, I fear.
My enemies shall know I am a queen,

The spouse of God, most high, most dear.

This armor I shall keep while life shall last;
Thou, Thou, hast given it Me, my King, my Spouse!
My fairest, brightest gems, by naught on earth surpast,
Shall be my sacred vows.

My first dear sacrifice, O Poverty,
Thou shalt go with me till my dying hour.
Detached from all things must the athlete be,
If he the race would run, and prove his power

Taste, worldly men! regret, remorse and pain,
The bitter fruits of earthly, vain desire;
The glorious palms of Poverty I gain,
I who to God alone aspire.

"Who would My heavenly Kingdom have from Me,
He must use violence," so Jesus said.
Ah well then! Poverty my mighty lance shall be,
The helmet for my head.

The pure white Angels' sister now am I;
My vow of Chastity has made me so.
Ah, how I hope one day with them to fly!
Meanwhile to daily combat must I go.
For my great Spouse, of every lord the Lord,
Struggle must I, with neither truce nor rest;
And Chastity shall be my heavenly sword.
To win men's souls to Jesus' breast.

O Chastity, my sword invincible!
To overcome my foes thou hast sufficed;
By thee am I --O joy ineffable!
The Spouse of Jesus Christ.

The proud, proud angel, in the realms of light,
Cried out, rebellious: "I will not obey!"
But I shall cry, throughout earth's dreary night,
"With all my heart, I will obey alway!"

With holy boldness all my soul is steeled,
Against hell's wild attacks I bravely dart;
Obedience is my firm and mighty shield,
The buckler on my valiant heart.
O conquering God! no other prize I seek,
Than to submit with all my heart to Thee;
Of victories th' obedient man shall speak
Through all eternity.
If now a soldier's weapon I can wield,
If valiantly like him the foe I face,
I also long to sing upon the field,
As sang the glorious Virgin of all grace.
Thou mak'st the chords to vibrate of Thy lyre.
That lyre, O Jesus! is my loving heart;
To sing Thy mercies is that heart's desire.
How sweet, how strong, how dear, Thou art.

With radiant smile, Thou Spouse, my heart's Delight,
I go to meet all foes from hell's dark land;
And singing I shall die, upon the field of fight,
My weapons in my hand.
March 25, 1897.

MY PEACE AND MY JOY.

How many souls on earth there are,
Who vainly seek for peace and rest!
With me, 'tis otherwise by far;
Joy dwells forever in my breast.
No fading blossom is this flower,
Of its decay no fear have I;
Like fragrant rose in springtime's bower
So fair it is, yet shall not die.

Wellnigh too great my gladness is,
All things I wish are mine today.
How can I help but show my bliss,
Who am so light at heart, so gay?
My joy I find in pain and loss,
I love the thorns that guard the rose;

With joy I kiss each heavy cross,
And smile with every tear that flows.

When clouds the sunny skies o'ercast,
And weary grows my heart the while,
My joy it is that joy is past,
And gone my Lord's consoling smile.
My peace is hid in Jesus' breast, -
May His sweet will alone be done!
What fear can mar my perfect rest,
Who love the shadow as the sun?

My peace, 'tis like a child to be,
That doth not plan, nor understand;
So, when I fall, Christ raiseth me,
And leads me gently by the hand.
My childish love I manifest,
And for His grace alone implore;
Then, if He hide, my love to test,
I only love Him all the more.

My peace, it is to hide my tears,
Nor ever show my bitter pain.
What joy to suffer through the years;
To veil with flowers each galling chain!
To suffer, yet make no complaint,
Since this, my Jesus, pleases Thee!
Could any trial make me faint?
'Tis Thy sweet cross is laid on me.

My peace, - it is with God to plead,
In prayers and tears, by day and night;
For many souls to intercede,
And say to Him, my heart's Delight:
"O Little Brother, Heavenly King!
For Thee the cross I gladly bear.
My only joy is suffering,
Since thus Thy earthly lot I share."

I long would live an exile here,
If that be Thy dear will for me;
Or soon would flee from exile drear,
If thou shouldst call me unto Thee.
Since Love's divine, celestial breath
Is all I need, my heart to bless,
What matters life, what matters death?
Love is my peace, my happiness!

    January 21, 1897

A LILY AMIDST THORNS.

FOR A NOVICE.

O King majestic, strong! e'en from my earliest days
, I well may call myself Thy work of grace alone;
Thy love to pay with love, Thy care to tell with praise,
I come with joy today, before Thy altar throne.
Jesu, my Best Beloved! what privilege is this?
For nothingness am I. What have I done for Thee?
Yet, clad in virginal white, it is today my bliss
To follow Thee, the Lamb, in heavenly ecstasy.

I know, alas, too well, that I am less than naught,
Weakness itself, and poor; devoid of virtues great
And yet Thou knowest well that I have always sought
With longing heart, Thyself; on Thee alone I wait
When my young heart first felt the fire of love burn bright,
Thou cam'st, O Christ! that fire to Thee alone to take;
Naught could content my soul but Thee, my one Delight; -
The Infinite alone my burning thirst could slake.

Like some wee lamb afar from its safe sheltering fold,
Gayly I played, and nothing knew of dangers drear.
Shepherdess, Queen of Heaven! thy mother love untold,
Thy mother watchfulness, drew me thy heart anear.
So, playing on the brink of pitfalls dread and deep,
Afar I saw the hill of Carmel beckon me;
And I divined that they who climb its summits steep,

Shall learn of love, to fly to heaven's eternity.

An angel's purity, dear Lord, attracts Thy heart,
An angel white as snow, in heaven's celestial mirth.
Dost thou not also love a lily kept apart
For Thee, from mire and taint; as white as snow, on earth?
If he, within Thy sight, exults all dazzling pure,
In brilliant stainless robes, whose lustre blinds our gaze,
Hast Thou not kept my robe as safe, as white, as sure?
My virgin heart has been the treasure of my days.

A WITHERED ROSE.

Jesus, when Thou didst leave Thy Mother's fond embrace,
Let go her hand;
And first, on our hard earth, Thy little foot didst place,
And trembling stand;
Within Thy pathway, then fresh rose leaves would I spread, -
Their Maker's dower, -
That so Thy tiny feet might very softly tread
Upon a flower.

These scattered rose leaves form true image of a soul,
O Child most dear!
That longs to immolate itself, complete and whole,
Each moment here.
On Thy blest altars, Lord, fresh roses fain would shine,
Radiant, near Thee;
They gladly give themselves. Another dream is mine,-
To fade for Thee!

How gaily decks Thy feasts, dear Child, a rose newblown,
Fragrant and fair!
But withered roses are forgot, -the wild winds' own,-
Cast anywhere.
Their scattered leaves seek now no earthly joy or pelf;
For self, no gain.
Ah, little Jesus! so, I give Thee all! Of self,
Let naught remain.

These roses trampled lie beneath the passer's tread,
Unmarked, unknown.
I comprehend their lot;-these leaves, though pale and dead,
Are still Thine own.
For Thee they die; as I my time, my life, my all
Have spent for Thee.
Men think a fading rose am I, whose leaves must fall
At death's decree.

For Thee I die, for Thee, Jesus, Thou Fairest Fair! -
Joy beyond telling!
Thus, fading, would I prove my love beyond compare,
All bliss excelling.
Beneath Thy feet, Thy way to smooth, through life's long night,
My heart would lie;
And softening Thy hard path up Calvary's awful height,
I thus would die.

    May, 1897

ABANDONMENT.

"Abandonment is the delicious fruit of love."
    St. Augustine.

I saw upon this earth
A marvelous tree arise;
Its vigorous root had birth,
O wonder! in the skies.
Never, beneath its shade,
Can aught disturb or wound;
There tempests are allayed,
There perfect rest is found
And love men call this tree,
From heaven's high portals sent;
Its fruit, how fair to see!
Is named abandonment.

What banquet here doth greet
Each reverent, hungry guest!

How, by its odors sweet,
The spirit is refreshed!
If we its fruit but touch,
Joy seems on us to pour.
Oh, taste, - for never such
A feast was yours before.
In this tumultuous world
It brings us perfect peace;
Though storms be round us hurled,
Its quiet shall not cease.
Abandonment gives rest
In Thee, O Jesus Christ!
Here is the food most blest
That has Thy saints sufficed.
Spouse of my soul, draw nigher!
I give my all to Thee.
What more can I desire
Than Thy sweet Face to see?
Naught can I do but smile,
Safe folded to Thy breast.
They who have known no guile
Find there most perfect rest.

As looks the floweret small
Up to the glorious sun,
So I, though least of all,
Seek my Beloved One.
King Whom I love the most!
The star I always see
Is Thy White Sacred Host,
Little and low like me;
And its celestial power,
Down from Thy altar sent,
Wakes in my heart that flower, -
Perfect abandonment.

All creatures here below,
At times, they weary me;
And willingly I go,
With God alone to be.

And if, sometimes, dear Lord,
Of me Thou weariest,
I wait upon Thy word;
Thy holy will is best.
Smiling, I wait in peace,
Till Thou return to me;
And never shall they cease, -
My songs of love for Thee.
All pain I now despise,
Naught can disquiet me;
Swifter than eagle flies,
My spirit flies to Thee.
Beyond the gloomy cloud,
Ever the skies are fair,
And angels sing aloud,
And God is reigning there.
And yet without a tear
I wait that bliss above,
Who in the Host have here
The perfect fruit of love.

Second Part

THE DEW DIVINE.

First Poem of Sister Teresa.

My sweetest Jesus! on Thy Mother's breast
Thy little Face is radiant with love;
Deign to reveal to me the mystery blest
That drew Thee down to exile from above.
Let me hide with Thee 'neath her veil of snow,
That now conceals Thee from all human sight.
Alone with Thee, bright Morning Star, I'll know
On earth a foretaste of heaven's deep delight.

When dawn awakens in the far off cast,
And first the sunbeams strike athwart the skies,
Looks for a precious balm - its daily feast
The unfolding floweret with expectant eyes.
Those spotless pearls of clear translucent dew
Are full of some mysterious vital power;
They form the sap that ever doth renew
And ope the petals of the half blown flower.

Thou art the Flower with petals still unclosed;
I gaze upon Thy beauty undefiled.
Thou art the Rose of Sharon long foretold,
Still in Thy glorious bud, Thou heavenly Child!
Thy dearest Mother's arms, so pure and white,
Form for Thee now a royal cradle throne;
Thy morning sun is Mary's bosom bright,
Thy sunlit dew her viqinal milk, my Own!

Ah, little Brother, shielded safe from harms,
In Thy deep eyes Thy future clear I see,--
Soon Thou wilt leave for us Thy Mother's arms;
E'en now to suffer, Love is urging Thee.
And round Thy very Cross, Thou fading Flower,
Still clings the fragrance of Thy cradle throne;
I recognize the pearls of Thy first hour:

This Blood drew life from Mary's milk, my Own.

Those pearly dews on all our altars rest;
The angels fain would slake their thirst thereby,
Offering to God these words, forever blest:
"Behold the Lamb "--St. John's adoring cry.
Yes, see the Word, made Bread for famished men,
The Eternal Priest, the Lamb on altar throne!
Since God's own Son is Mary's Son, all, then,
This Bread drew life from Mary's milk, my Own!

On love divine, on joy, on glory's light,
The seraphs feast with rapture ever new;
I, a frail child, in the ciborium bright
See but a milk white Host, like pearly dew.
And since 'tis milk that suits with childhood most,
And Thou art Love Itself upon Thy throne,
So, tender Love, in my white daily Host
I see Thy Mother's virginal milk, my Own!
   February 2, 1893

TO OUR LADY OF VICTORIES.

QUEEN OF VIRGINS, OF APOSTLE`S,
AND OF MARTYRS.

O Mother! thou my heart's desire
Hast granted now; so hear my cry
Of gratitude and love like fire
Thy child uplifts to thee on high.

By love for God and all mankind,
By bonds of prayer and earnest will,
Thou deignest now my soul to bind
To those who Christ's last wish fulfil.

'Tis theirs through pagan lands to go,
And raise the cross of Christ on high;
'Tis mine, within the cloister low,
His slightest will to satisfy.

I long for suffering; and the cross
With strong desire my heart doth crave.
A thousand deaths were gain, not loss,
If but one soul I help to save!

For this to Carmel's hill I've come,
Myself to immolate for men.
Christ brought a fire from Heaven's high dome
I fain would light in hearts again.

Where Afric suns the desert bake,
Where Asian Su-tchen* fronts the east,
My Mother, I can help to make
Thy virginal name revered and blest.

* Countries evangelized by her "brothers," the missionaries.

My prayers shall travel every day,
As fast as mighty river rolls;
My brothers, missioned far away,
Helped here by me, shall conquer souls;

And so the pure baptismal stream
Shall make of many a Pagan child
A temple, where God's grace shall beam,
And God with man be reconciled.

Ah! might I see dear children fill
The heavenly courts where seraphs sing!
Them, by my prayers and God's sweet will,
My brothers shall to Jesus bring.

The palm my spirit longs to gain,
My brother's hand in mine shall place.
A martyr's sister! Any pain
Would seem delight to win that grace.

The fruit of our apostolate
Our longing eyes at last shall see,
When, pressing on through heaven's gate,

Our souls shall meet the saved and Thee.

Be theirs the honor of the fight,
My priestly brothers far away
Be mine, reflection of their light,
At last, in heaven's eternal day!

1897

THE QUEEN OF HEAVEN TO HER LITTLE MARY.

To A Postulant Named Mary

Could I some childlike spirit see,
Resembling Christ, my little Child,
Then she with Him should cradled be
Upon my bosom undefiled.

Angelic spirits, hovering near,
Would envy such celestial bliss;
Yet Thee I chose, so come then, dear!
My Child awaits thy timid kiss.

Oh, Jesus' sister thou shalt be,
I choose thee for "this better part."
Wilt gladly bear Him company?
Then shalt thou rest upon my heart.
And I will shield thee 'neath my veil,
Near Bethlehem's Babe so fair and bright.
Oh, thou shalt think the stars are pale,
Compared with this divine delight.

But would'st forever stay with me,
And with this Christ-Child, in my care?
Then thou all fitly dressed must be
In childhood's graces heavenly fair.

Upon thy brow mine eyes must trace
Thy light of purity divine;
Simplicity's most tender grace

Through all things in thy life must shine.

God, Three in One, and One in Three,
By angels tremblingly adored,
Asks gently to be called by thee
"Flower of the Fields," that simple word.

As fair white daisies lift their face
With steadfast meekness to the skies,
So thou must look with kindred grace
Within the Christ Child's holy eyes.

To worldly men no charm appears
In this meek King Who wears no crown.
Thou oft shalt see the burning tears
From Jesus' eyes fail swiftly down.

Then thine own pains thou must forget,
To calm and soothe our Blessed One;
Then thou must prize the vows that set
Thy place so close to Him alone.

Our God, Whose mighty power controls
Fury of flood and force of flame,
Now lieth low, to save men's souls,
A Child enclothed in our shame.

The Word, the Father's Word on high,
My little Lamb, thy Brother dear,
Now speaks no word, He breathes no sigh;
Silent and dumb He lieth here.

That silence forms the mystic sign
Of love beyond all utterance deep;
Its meaning thou must well divine
And day by day like silence keep.

And if, at times, His eyelids close,
Rest then near Him in perfect peace;
His Sacred Heart no slumber knows,

His love for thee shall never cease.

Nor think, dear Mary, anxiously,
About the task of every day;
To love thy blessed work shall be,
Its holy crown be thine for aye.

Lo! if some voice reproaches thee
Because no great things thou hast done,
Oh, make this answer steadfastly:
"But I loved much!" So heaven is won.

Our Lord Himself thy crown shall weave;
And if thou seek His love alone,
If all for Him thou gladly leave,
Near His for aye shall be thy throne.

When life's long vigil is all past,
Heav'n's dawn shall break in joy for thee;
And face to face, at last, at last,
The Vision of God shall welcome thee!

   Christmas 1894

WHY I LOVE THEE MARY.

Last Poem Of Sister Teresa

Fain would I sing, O Mother blest! the reasons why I love thee;
Why e'en to name thy name, with joy, O Mary! fills my heart;
And why the glorious thoughts of thee, in greatness far above me,
Inspire no fear within my soul, so dear and sweet thou art.
Yet, if I were to see thee now, in majesty stupendous,
Surpassing all the crowned saints in highest heaven above,
Scarce could I dream I am thy child, (O truth sublime, tremendous!),
For I should think myself to be unworthy of thy love.

The mother, who desires to be her child's best earthly treasure,
Must ever share its grief with it, must understand its pain.
Queen of my heart! how many years, thy sorrows had no measure;

What bitter tears thine eyes have shed, my worthless heart to gain!
So, musing on thy earthly life, in Scripture's sacred story,
I dare to look upon thy face, and unto thee draw nigh;
For when I see thee suffering,-concealed thy marvelous glory-
It is not hard, then, to believe thy little child am I.

When Gabriel came from heaven's courts, to ask thee to be mother
Of God Who reigns omnipotent to all eternity,
I see thee, Mary! then prefer to that great grace, another,
Through all thy consecrated life a virgin pure to be.
And so I now can comprehend, immaculate white maiden!
Why thou wast dearer unto God than heaven itself could be;
And how thy humble, human frame, with mortal weakness laden,
Could yet contain the Eternal Word, Love's vast unbounded Sea.

I love thee when I hear thee call thyself the handmaid only
Of God, Whom thou didst win to earth by thy humility;
All-powerful it made thee then, above all women, lonely,
And drew, into thy bosom chaste, the Blessed Trinity,
The Holy Spirit, Love Divine, o'ershadowed thee, O Mother!
And God the Father's only Son incarnate was in thee.
How many sinful, sorrowing souls shall dare to call Him - Brother!
For He shall be called: Jesus, thy first-born, eternally.

And oh! despite my frailties, dear Mary! well thou knowest
That I at times, like thee, possess the Almighty in my breast.
Shall I not tremble at the gift, O God! that Thou bestowest ?
A mother's treasure is her child's: - I still my fears to rest.
For I, O Mary, am thy child! O Mother dear and tender.
Shall not thy virtues and thy love plead now with God for me?
Then, when the pure white sacred Host, in all its veiled splendor,
Visits my heart, thy spotless Lamb will think He comes to thee.

Oh, thou dost help me to believe that e'en for us, frail mortals,
'Tis not impossible to walk where we thy footsteps see;
The narrow road before us now, thou lightest to heaven's portals.
Who lowliest virtues here below didst practise perfectly.
Near thee, O Mother! I would stay, little, unknown and lowly;
Of earthly glory, oh! how plain I see the vanity!
In the house of St. Elizabeth, thy cousin dear and holy,

I learn of thee to practise well most ardent charity.

There, too, I listen on my knees, great Queen of all the Angels!
To that sweet canticle that flows in rapture from thy soul;
So dost thou teach me how to sing like heavenly, glad evangels
And glorify my Jesus, Who alone can make me whole.
Thy burning words of love divine are mystic flowers victorious,
Whose fragrance shall embalm the long, long, ages yet to be.
In thee, indeed, the Almighty King hath done great things and glorious!
I meditate upon them now, and bless my God in thee.

When good St. Joseph did not know the great archangel's story,
Which thou wouldst fain conceal from men in thy humility,
O tabernacle of the Lord! thou didst not tell thy glory,
But veiled the Saviour's presence in profoundest secrecy,
Thy silence, how I love it now, so eloquent, so moving!
For me it is a concert sweet, of melody sublime;
I learn thereby the grandeur of a soul that God is proving,
That only looks for help from Him and in His chosen time.

Then later still, O Joseph! and O Mary! I behold you
Repulsed in little Bethlehem by all the dwellers there;
From door to door you vainly went, for all the people told you
They had no place to shelter you, no time to give you care.
Their rooms were for the great alone; and in a stable dreary
The Queen of Heaven gave birth to Him Who made both heaven and earth.
O Mother of my Saviour! then, thou wast not sad nor weary;
In that poor shed how grand thou wert! how painless was that Birth!

And there when, wrapped in swaddling bands, I see the King Eternal,
When of the Word divine, supreme, the feeble cry I hear
O Mary, can I envy e'en the angels' joy supernal?
The Master Whom they worship is My little Brother dear.
What praises must I give to thee, who, in earth's gloomy prison,
Brought forth this lovely heaven-sent Flower, before our eyes to bloom!
Though unto shepherds and wise men a star had grandly risen,
These things were kept within thy heart as in some secret room.

I love thee when I see thee next, like other Hebrew women,
To Israel's temple turn thy steps when dawned the fortieth day;

I love thee yielding humbly up, to aged, favored Simeon,
The Lord Who should redeem us all when years had fled away.
And first my happy smiles awake, to hear his glorious singing,--
That "Nunc Dimittis" that shall ring till Time itself shall die;
But soon those joyous notes are changed, and my hot tears are springing;--
"A sword of grief must be thy lot," thus runs his prophecy.

O Queen of all the martyr-host! till thy life here is ended,
That sharp, sharp sword shall pierce thy heart! At once, it pierces sore.
That thy dear Child from Herod's wrath may surely be defended,
I see thee as an exile fled to Egypt's pagan shore.
Beneath thy veil thy Jesus slept, thy peace no fears were daunting,
When Joseph came to bid thee wake, and straightway flee from home;
And then at once I see thee rise, as called by angels chanting,
Content, without a questioning word, in foreign lands to roam.

In Egypt and in poverty, I think I see thee, Mary,
All glad at heart, all radiant, with joy beyond compare.
What matters exile unto thee? Thy true home cannot vary.
Hast thou not Jesus, with thee still? and with Him Heaven is there.
But, oh! in fair Jerusalem, a sorrow, vast, unbounded,
Indeed o'erwhelmed thy mother-heart with grief beyond compare
For three days Jesus hid Himself; no word to thee was spoken.
Thou truly wast an exile then, and knew what exiles bear.

And when, at last, thine eyes again were thy Son's face beholding,
And love entranced thee, watching Him among the doctors wise,
"My Child!" thou saidst, "now tell me why didst leave my arms enfolding?
Didst Thou not know we sought for Thee with tear-endimmed eyes?
The Child-God answered to thee then, to thy sweet, patient wooing,
O Mother whom He loved so well, whose heart was well-nigh broken!
"How is it that you sought for Me? Wist not I must be doing
My Father's work?" Oh, who shall sound the depths those words betoken?

But next the Gospel tells me that, in His hidden mission,
Subject to Joseph and to thee was Christ, the Holy Boy;
And then my heart reveals to me how true was His submission,
And how beyond all words to tell, thy daily, perfect joy.
And now the temple's mystery I understand, dear Mother!
The answer, and the tone of voice, of Christ, my King adored.

'Twas meant the pattern thou shouldst be, thereafter to all other
Tried souls who seek, in Faith's dark night the coming of the Lord.

Since Heaven's high King has willed it so His Mother and His dearest
Should know the anguish of that night the torn heart's deepest woe,
Then are not those, who suffer thus, to Mary's heart the nearest?
And is not love in suffering God's highest gift below?
All, all that He has granted me, oh! tell Him He may take it!
Tell Him, dear Mother! He may do whate'er He please with me;
That He may bruise my heart today, and make it sore, and break it,
So only through Eternity my eyes His Face may see!

I know, indeed, at Nazareth, O Virgin rich in graces!
As the lowly live, so thou didst live, and sought no better things;
Of ecstasies and wonders there, our eyes can find no traces,
O thou who daily dwelt beside the incarnate King of Kings!
On earth, we know, is very great the number of the lowly;
With neither fear nor trembling now we dare to look on thee.
By common lot and humble path, our Mother dear and holy,
Thou wast content to walk to heaven, and thus our guide to be.

Through all my weary exile here, I fain would walk beside thee.
O my pure and precious Mother! be near to me each day!
Thy beauty thrills my heart with joy. Deign now to guard and guide me!
What depths of love are in thy heart for me thy child, alway!
Before thy kind maternal glance, my many fears are banished;
Thou teachest me to gently weep, and then to sing for joy;
Thou dost not scorn our happy days, nor hast thou wholly vanished;
Thou smilest on us tenderly, as once upon thy Boy!

When bride and groom at Cana's feast knew well the wine was failing,
And knew not whence to bring supply, their need thine eyes perceived,
To Christ, the Master, thou didst speak, who knew His power availing,
The Maker of created things, in Whom thy soul believed.
But first He seemed thy mother-heart's kind prayer to be denying.
"What matters this, O woman! unto Me and thee?" said He.
But "Mother," in His soul's deep depths, His filial heart was crying;
And that first miracle He wrought, Mother, He wrought for thee.

One day, while sinners crowded round to hear what He was saying,

In His desire to save their souls and them to heaven beguile,
Lo! thou wast there amid the throng, and thou wast meekly praying
That they would let thee nearer come, and speak with Him awhile.
And then thy Son spoke out this word mysterious like that other.
To show us thus His marvelous love for all the souls of men;
He said: "Who is My brother, and My sister, and My Mother?
'Tis he who does My Father's will!" The Father's will, again!

O Virgin, pure, immaculate! O Mother, tenderest, dearest!
Hearing these words that Jesus spake, this time thou wast not grieved.
No! thy great heart it leaped for joy, O thou His friend the nearest!
Because our longing souls likewise to kinship He received.
Oh, how thy heart is glad to know His love to us is given,
The treasure, that cannot be weighed, of His Divinity!
Who shall not love thee well today, and bless thee in high heaven,
Seeing thy tender care for us, thy generosity!
For truly thou dost love us all as thy Child Jesus loves us;
And for our sake thou didst consent to stay when He had risen.
Since, if we love, then all to give, e'en self, both tries and proves us,
So thou, to prove thy love, didst stay in earth's dark, dreary prison.
Thy love for souls our Saviour knew, that love His heart had sounded;
He left thee to us when He went to God's right hand on high.
Refuge of sinners! on thy prayers how many hopes are grounded!
Christ gave thee to us from His cross; for us He hears thy cry.

For thou -His Mother- there didst stand, that awful day, on Calvary;
As a priest before God's altar, at the cross so thou didst stand.
And to appease the Father's wrath, didst offer up, O Mary!
Thy Jesus, our Emmanuel, at God's supreme command.
A prophet had foretold this thing, O Mother brokenhearted!
"Is any sorrow like to thine?" Thy grief no words can say!
Blest Queen of martyrs! left on earth when Jesus had departed!
'Twas thy heart's blood for us was given on that unequalled day.

Henceforth thy shelter in thy woe was St. John's humble dwelling;
The son of Zebedee replaced the Son Whom heaven adored.
Naught else the Gospels tell us of thy life, in grace excelling;
It is the last they say of thee, sweet Mother of my Lord!
But that deep silence, oh! I think it means that, up in glory,
When time is past, and into heaven thy children safe are come,

The Eternal Word, my Mother dear, Himself will tell thy story,
To charm our souls, thy children's souls, in our eternal home.
Soon I shall hear that harmony, that blissful, wondrous singing;
Soon, soon, to heaven that waits for us, my soul shall swiftly fly.

O Thou who cam'st to smile on me at dawn of life's beginning!
Come once again to smile on me.... Mother! the night is nigh.
I fear no more thy majesty, so far, so far above me,
For, I have suffered sore with thee; now hear my heart's deep cry!
Oh! let me tell thee face to face, dear Virgin! how I love thee;
And say to thee forevermore: thy little child am I.

    May 1897

Third Part

TO MY GUARDIAN ANGEL

O glorious guardian of my frame!
In heaven's high courts thou shinest bright,
As some most pure and holy flame,
Before the Lord of endless light.
Yet for my sake thou com'st to earth,
To be my brother, Angel dear:
My friend and keeper from my birth,
By day and night to me most near.

Knowing how weak a child am I,
By thy strong hand thou guidest me;
The stones that in my pathway lie,
I see thee move them carefully.
Ever thy heavenly tones invite
My soul to look to God alone;
And ever grows thy face more bright,
When I more meek and kind have grown.

O thou who speedest through all space
More swiftly than the lightnings fly!
Go very often, in my place,
To those I love most tenderly.
With thy soft touch, oh! dry their tears;
Tell them the cross is sweet to bear;
Speak my name softly in their ears,
And Jesu's name, supremely fair.

Through all my life, though brief it be,
I fain would succor souls from sin.
Dear Angel, sent from heaven to me,
Kindle thy zeal my heart within!
Naught but my holy poverty,
And daily cross to give have I;
O join them to thine ecstasy,
And offer them to God on high.

Thine are heaven's glory and delight,
The riches of the King of kings;
The Host in our ciboriums bright
Is mine, and all the wealth pain brings.
So with the Cross, and with the Host,
And with thine aid, dear Angel Friend,
I wait in peace, on time's dark coast,
Heaven's happiness that knows no end.

    February, 1897

TO MY LITTLE BROTHERS IN HEAVEN
THE HOLY INNOCENTS

"The Lord shall gather together the lambs with His arm, and shall take them up in His bosom." Is. 40:11. Happy those whom God regards as justified without works! for to him that worketh, the reward is not reckoned according to grace, but according to debt." It is, then, gratuitously that those who do no works are justified by grace, in virtue of the Redemption of which Jesus Christ is the Author. Romans 4: 4, 5 ,6.

O happy little ones! with what sweet tenderness
The King of Heaven
Blessed you, when here below! How often His caress
To you was given!
You were the type of all the Innocents to come.
In dreams I know
The boundless joy the King gives you in heaven's high home,
He loves you so!

Before earth's bitter griefs, dear lilies of the Lord,
Had dimmed your eyes,
You had beheld the gifts,- how very beauteous! -- stored
In Paradise.
O fragrant buds, soon plucked at day's sweet dawning bright,
By God's own hand;
His Sacred Heart is now the Sun by Whose soft light
Those buds expand!

What perfect care and oh! what ceaseless watchfulness,

What love alway,
Lavishes on you here our Mother Church, to bless
Souls of a day!
In her maternal arms, you were in holy rite
To Jesus given;
And through eternity, you will be the delight
Of His fair Heaven.

Dear little ones! you join the virginal court, in state
Following the Lamb;
And you the sweet new song shall sing (O privilege great!)
Unto His Name.
You to the conqueror's palm, without the deadly fight,
Have safely come.
O charming victors: Christ from you has taken all blight, And brought you home.

It needs no precious stones, all luminous and gay,
To deck your hair;
The lustre of your curls, sweet Innocents, today,
Makes Heaven more fair.
To you grand martyrs lend their palms; they give their crowns,
Your brows to grace;
Upon their knees you find, dear children, now your thrones,
In their embrace.

In splendid courts on high, with tiny cherub throngs
Gayly you play:
Beloved baby band! your childish sports and songs
Charm heaven alway.
God tells you how He makes the birds, the flowers, the snow,
The sunlight clear;
No genius here below knows half the things you know,
O children, dear!

From Heaven's azure vault you tear the veils that make
Such mystery:
The glowing myriad stars in your wee hands you take,
Your toys to be.
Running Heaven's highways, there, your tiny footsteps leave

A silvery trace;
In the bright Milky Way, I think I see, at eve,
Each shining face.

To Mary's welcoming arms, when your gay games are done,
How swift you hie!
Hiding beneath her veil your heads like Christ Her Son
In sleep you lie.
Heaven's darling little pets! audacity like this
Delights our Lord;
And you can even dare caress and gently kiss
His Face adored.

That Blessed Lord has deigned you for my pattern here
To give to me;
O Holy Innocents, like you so pure and dear
I strive to be.
Pray, pray, that I may gain all childhood's graces best,-
Your candor true,
Your sweet abandonment, your innocence so blest,
That charm my view!

Thou, of my exiled soul, O Lord! full well dost know
The ardent prayer.
Fair Lily of the Vale, on Thee I would bestow Earth's lilies fair;
These buds of spring I love, and long to find for Thee,
Thou King adored!
Grant the baptismal grace to each one tenderly;
Then cull them, Lord!

My pains and my joys I offer with delight,-
For children's souls:
Thus to augment Thy ranks of Innocents most white,
The while time rolls;
And, 'mongst these Innocents, I ask Thee that it place
To me be given.
Grant to me, as to them, Thy kiss, O wondrous grace
Jesus! in Heaven.

    February, 1897

THE MELODY OF ST. CECILIA.

"During the sound of the instruments, Cecilia was singing in her heart."

-- Office of the Church.

Thou glorious Saint of God! in ecstasy I see
The path of shining light thy footsteps left below;
And still I think I hear thy heavenly melody;
Of thy celestial chant e'en here the sounds we know.
Now, of my exiled soul, accept the fervent prayer;
Upon thy virginal heart let my young heart find rest!
Almost unequalled here wast thou, O lily fair,
Immaculately pure, and how divinely blest!

Most chaste white dove of Rome! through all thy life on earth
No other spouse than Christ thy heart desired to find.
He chose thy favored soul, e'en from thy hour of birth,
And made it rich in grace and virtues all combined.
And yet a mortal came, on fire with youth and pride;
He saw how sweet thou wert, thou white celestial flower!
And then, to gain thy love - to win thee for his bride-
He strove with all his strength, from that momentous hour.
Soon bridal feasts he spread, his palace decked with glory,
Bade minstrels play their best, and songs ring loudly there,
While still thy virginal heart sang soft thy Saviour's story,
Whose echo rose to heaven like incense sweet and rare.

How couldst thou sing, so far from Heaven, thy fatherland,
When seeing near thy side, that mortal bold and frail ?
Did not thy heart crave, then, in heaven's high courts to stand,
And dwell, forever safe, with Christ beyond the veil?
But no! thy harp I hear vibrate like seraph's singing,
Harp of thy love, whose sound so softly smote the car;
These words, to Christ thy Lord, in thy sweet chant were ringing:
"Now keep my young heart pure, O Jesus, Spouse most dear."
Abandonment how true! O wondrous melody!
By that celestial chant thy love now stands revealed
The love that knows no fear, but sleeps in ecstasy
Upon the Saviour's Heart, from every ill concealed.

In wide blue skies appeared the radiant white star
That came, to lighten up, with meek and timid glow,
The luminous night that shows, unveiled to us afar,
That virginal love, in heaven, which virgin spouses know.

But here, Valerian dreamed of earthly joy and bliss.
Cecilia! thou alone wast his young heart's desire.
Ah, when thy hand he gained, he gained far more than this!
That hand showed him a path to better things, and higher.
"O friend! " to him thou saidst "near me doth watch alway
An angel of the Lord, who keeps me pure as snow,
Who leaves me not alone, neither by night nor day;
E'en in my sleep, his wings protect from harm and woe.
At night, his holy face, with clear and silvery light
A glory lovelier far than morning sun,- doth shine.
That face to me appears like some blest image bright,
Transparent, marvelous, of God's own face divine."
Then cried Valerian: " Show me this angel blest,
That I may give my faith to thy firm word, fair maid;
Or else believe that hate for thee will fill my breast,
And thou, before my wrath, shalt shudder sore afraid."

O dove, within the rock of God's strong heart concealed,
No fear hadst thou, that night, of subtlest fowler's snare:
The Face of Jesus, then, Its light to thee revealed;
His sacred gospels lay upon thy bosom fair.
"Valerian!" that word was said with gentlest smile,
"My heavenly guide, who hears, will answer thy request.
Soon thou his face shalt see; his voice shall thee beguile,
For martyrdom to seek, and thus to find thy rest.
But, ere his face thou see, baptismal grace must make
Thy soul as white as snow, that God therein may dwell.
The one true God Himself thy heart His home shall make,
The Spirit give thee life, that thou mayst serve Him well;
The Word, the Father's Son, and Son of Mary chaste,
Must immolate Himself, in His vast love for thee,
Upon His altar throne; and there thou must be placed,
Beside that throne, to feed on Him Who died for thee.

Then shall the seraph bright, thee for his brother, claim,
And, seeing in thy heart the home of God his King,
Thee shall he lift from earth's dark dens of sin and shame;
Thee, to his own abode, that angel then shall bring."
"Ah! in my heart I feel a new fire burn tonight!"
Transformed by God's own grace, the young patrician cried.
Oh! come, within my soul to dwell, Thou Lord of light!
Worthy my love shall be of thee, Cecile, my bride!"

In his baptismal robe, the type of innocence,
Valerian, at last, the angel's face beheld;
In awe he gazed upon that grave magnificence;
That radiant, crown decked brow his old ambitions quelled.
Fresh roses in his hands did that grand spirit bear,
Pure lilies, dazzling white, to his strong heart he pressed.
In gardens of high heaven had bloomed those blossoms rare,
Beneath the rays of love from their Creator blest.

"O Spouses dear to Heaven! the martyrs' royal rose
Shall crown your brows," exclaimed that angel from on high
"No voice on earth can sing, no mortal tongue disclose,
Its value beyond price, that lasts eternally.
I lose myself in God, His attributes proclaim;
But I cannot, for Him, bear pain, though fain would I!
I cannot shed or tears or blood for His dear name;
To prove my love for Him, I cannot gladly die.
Oh! purity is ours, the angels' special grace,-
Our vast, unbounded joy, that ne'er shall fade away;
But o'er our lofty lot yours hath a loftier place,
For you -you can be pure, and you can die, today'

"Of chaste virginity, you see the emblem here,
In these white lilies sweet,- fair gift from Christ the Lamb;
The pure white crown He gives, in glory you shall wear;
And you for aye shall chant the new song to His name.
Your union, spotless, chaste, shall win great souls to God
Souls that no other spouse, than Christ, shall seek on earth;
And near His heavenly throne, when life's hard path is trod,
There you shall see them shine, in saintly joy and mirth."
Cecilia, lend to me thy melody most sweet:

How many souls would I convert to Jesus now.
I fain would die, like thee, to win them to His feet;
For him give all my tears, my blood. Oh, help me thou!
Pray for me that I gain, on this our pilgrim way
Perfect abandonment - that sweetest fruit of love.
Saint of my heart! oh, soon, bring me to endless day;
Obtain that I may fly, with thee, to heaven above!

    April 28, 1893

CANTICLE OF ST. AGNES

"My only Love is Christ."

From the Acts of her Martyrdom

Christ is my Love alone, all life is He for me;
He is my one Betrothed, Who charms my dazzled eyes;
E'en now I hear vibrate the solemn harmony
Of His melodious sighs.

With precious stones and gold He decks my flowing hair,
Already on my hand shines bright His nuptial ring;
And many lustrous stars, magnificently fair,
Are love gifts from my King.
With pearls, all price beyond, has He adorned my hands;
About my neck He placed a necklace wondrous bright;
Celestial rubies red, from far off unknown lands,
Bedeck my ears tonight.

Betrothed am I to Him on Whom the angels wait,
Trembling before His throne throughout eternity;
The sun and moon His praise with rapture will relate,
Till time shall cease to be.

Divine His Person is; heaven is His realm of bliss;
He for His Mother chose a Virgin here on earth;
Who no beginning hath, nor end, His Father is,--
Eternal is that birth.

Ah! when this Jesus Christ at times to touch I dare,
More pure becomes my heart; more chaste, dear Lord, am I!
The kisses of His mouth give me the treasure fair
Of blest virginity.

His signet He hath set already on my face,
That so no earthly love may dare draw nigh to me;
Kept thus for Christ alone, by His abiding grace,
His perfect purity.

Cleansed by the precious Blood He shed on Calvary's cross,
Already here I taste of heaven's matchless bliss;
The honey and the milk -with joys that know not loss-
Come to me with His kiss.

No thought of fear have I, of either flame or sword:
For naught can now disturb this perfect heavenly peace
A fire of love divine pervades my soul, O Lord:
And never shall it cease.

   January 21, 1896.

TO THE VENERABLE THEOPHANE VENARD, MARTYRED

O Theophane,* angelic martyr blest!
All the elect to sing thy praise aspire;
And thee to hail, behold! there stand confest
The Seraphim, with love divine on fire.
I, a poor exile still on this dull earth,
Can not with them my joyful song combine;
Yet will I take my harp, and sing thy worth,
And claim thee as a kindred soul to mine.

Thy brief bright sojourn here was like a psalm
Of heavenly melody, all hearts upraising;
Thy poet nature sang sweet songs like balm,
Through all thy life thy dearest Saviour praising.
Writing thy farewell thy last earthly night,
That farewell was a song of Spring and love,
"I, little butterfly, the first take flight,

Of all our loved ones, to our home above."

Thou, happy martyr! in the hour of death
Didst taste the deep delight of suffering:
Thou didst declare, e'en with thy dying breath,
That it is sweet to suffer for the King.

* Sister Teresa died in 1897, since then the Life of Theophane, beheaded for the faith at Tonquin in 1861, has become almost as well known as her own. These kindred souls in Heaven, have been inciting thousands of souls upon earth to spiritual heroism. He crying out for the Foreign Missions, she opening the road for Christ's little ones to run in the hidden ways of prayer and penance.

When the stern headsman made thee offer fair
Thy torture to abridge, how swift thy word:
"Oh, blest am I my Master's cup to share!
Long let my suffering last with Christ my Lord!"

O virginal lily! life had but begun,
When Jesus heard thy loving heart's desire.
I see in thee a flower whose race is run,
Yet his hand plucked it but to lift it higher.
And now, no longer, exile dost thou know;
Thy ecstasy the Blest exult to see.
Thou Rose of love! the Virgin white as snow
Rejoices in thy heavenly purity.

Soldier of Christ, thy armor lend to me!
For sinners' souls I long to give my life;
For them to give my tears, my blood, like thee:
Protect me then, and arm me for the strife!
For them I fain would fight, till life is done;- -
God's kingdom take by force, their souls to save.
"Not peace to earth I bring," (so spake God's Son),
"But fire and sword I bring." Oh, saving glaive!

How dear is now to me that pagan horde,
The object of thy burning love below
If Jesus would to me such grace accord,

Ah, thither with what ardor would I go.
Before Him space and distance fade away.
This earth is but a plaything on the breeze;
My actions, my small sufferings today,
Can make my Jesus loved beyond the seas.

Oh, were I but a fading springtime flower,
That soon the Lord would gather to His breast!
Come down, O Theophane, at my last hour;
Come down for me, thou youthful martyr blest!

Come, with the virginal flames of purest love,
Come, burn from out my soul all earthly clay,
That I may fly to heaven's courts above,
And join thy cohort in unending day.

       February 2, 1897.

Fourth Part

THE STORY OF A SHEPHERDESS
WHO BECAME QUEEN.

To a young Sister named Mary Magdalen, for her Profession day.

On this glad day, dear Magdalene,
We come to sing with praises due
The wonderful, strong, gentle chain
That binds your heavenly Spouse and you.
Oh, hear us tell the charming story
Of how a shepherdess once heard
A Monarch bid her share His glory,
And how she answered to his word.

The shepherdess sing,
Whom the Heavenly King
With glory crowned head
Doth here, this day, at Carmel, wed!

This shepherdess, so small, so poor,
While spinning, kept her flocks with care.
She loved the flowers beside her door,
The birds that fluttered here and there;
She knew what tongue the river spake,
The verdant woods, the skies above;
She loved them for her Master's sake,
As tokens of His boundless love.
But oh! she loved most tenderly
Jesus and Mary. All her heart
She gave, and they loved Melanie,
And came to speak with her apart.

"Will you," to her the sweet Queen said,
"Near me, on Carmel, come to dwell?
Will you be Magdalene, instead
Of Melanie, and serve God well?

"Child, quit your flock, seek God alone,

Nor mourn the lambs you ne'er shall see!
Upon this mountain all my own,
Jesus your only Lamb shall be."
"Oh, come! thy soul has charmed My sight,"
Spake Jesus, "Come, be thou My bride!
Who gave to God all earth's delight!
Come, reign forever at My side!"

Gladly the humble shepherdess
Responded to that gentle call;
And following Mary, swift to bless,
She came to Carmel's lofty wall.

'Tis you, O little Magdalene!
We feast with, on this joyous day!
The shepherdess is now a Queen,
Near Christ, her Spouse and King alway.

O! cherished Sister, you know well
To serve our God, it is to reign!
Our Jesus did not cease to tell
This lesson through His life of pain;
"Among the great, on heaven's height,
Who would stand first eternally
Must choose on earth the lowest place,
To hide from sight the least to be."

Happy are you, O Magdalene!
In your fixed lot in Carmel's home,
Can there, for you, be any pain
Who here so close to heaven come?

Both Martha's, Mary's is your part
To pray, to wait upon the Lord -
To love Him here with all your heart,
And have Him for your great reward.

Yet if, sometimes, sharp suffering
Shall come to flood your soul with night,

From out your pain will gladness spring
For God you suffer. What delight!
His tenderness, divine and sweet,
Shall make you very soon forget
The thorns that lie beneath your feet,
The tears with which your eyes were wet.

The angels envy you today!
They fain would taste your joy, Marie!
Your ecstasy, divinely gay
The spouse of Jesus Christ to be.
Soon, soon among the angel bands,
Among the Virtues, Thrones and Powers,
Your Spouse and King in heaven's bright lands
You, too, shall praise through endless hours.

This shepherdess soon,
So poor 'neath the moon,
In heaven a queen,
Beside her King shall yet be seen.

      November 20,1894.

PRAYER OF THE CHILD OF A SAINT.

TO HER GOOD FATHER, CALLED HOME TO GOD,
July 29, 1894.

Remember thou how once upon this earth
Thy joy was found in caring for us all!
Hear now the prayer of those who owe their birth
To thee, dear father; bless us when we call!
A little while ago, in Heaven, our home above,
Thou to our mother's side hast come with saintly love.
Together now ye reign,
in Heaven made one again.
O'er us keep guard!
Remember thy first born, thy bright Marie,
She who was dearest ever in thy sight;
Remember how her charm, her gaiety,

Her love, her goodness, filled thee with delight,
That daily source of joy thou didst renounce for God;
And thou didst bless the band, that made thee feel His rod.
Thy "diamond" bright and fair,
Thy rarest of the rare,

Remember thou!

* SISTER TERESA was the youngest of nine children, four of whom died in infancy, four became Carmelite nuns, and one a Visitation nun. These are the "nine lilies bright," referred to in the poem here as forming their saintly father's coronet in Heaven. He used to call Teresa his "little queen," Marie his "diamond," Pauline his "pearl." He died of paralysis, after months of helplessness, tended by Celine. These remarks serve to explain the poem.

Remember thou thy beautiful "pure pearl,"
The timid lamb once to thy tendence given!
Trusting in God, behold thy lovely girl
Guide Carmel's flock along the road to Heaven. Of thy beloved ones,
"Mother" is she today:
Then come to guide even now thy darling on her way!
This Carmel of Thine own
Remember at Heaven's throne,
Remember thou!

Remember now thy strong and ardent prayer
Made here for thy third child, thy Leonie!
God heard thee; for to her this earth so fair
But banishment and exile seems to be.
She, too, from this gay world, to God would turn aside;
She loves Him only, and becomes His bride.
Her ardent, burning sighs,
Her Heaven sent ecstasies,
Remember thou!

Remember thou thy faithful child, Celine,
Who was to thee like angel from the skies,
When close to thine the Face of Christ was seen,
Testing thy virtue by great sacrifice!
In Heaven thou reignest now; her task is past and gone;

Now unto Jesus Christ she gives her life alone.
Protect her future days,
Who very often says:
Remember thou!

And, oh! remember thou thy "little queen,"
The tender love with which her heart o'erflowed;
Remember where at first her steps have been,
And whose hand guided her along her road.

Papa, remember now, that in her infancy
Her innocence was given into God's care by thee.
Even her curling hair
To thee was dear and fair!
Remember thou!

Remember thou that on the terrace green
Her place was often on thy saintly knees;
And murmuring a prayer for her, "thy queen,"
Thou didst sing softly on the Sunday breeze,
And she, upon thy heart, saw in thy holy face
A shining of Heaven's light, a strange unearthly grace.
The beauty, sung by thee,
Was of eternity!
Remember thou!

Remember now that Sunday ever blest,
When thou a pure white flower to her didst give,
And to thy child, dose to thy bosom pressed,
Didst grant the grace on Carmel's hill to live.
Oh, father dear, recall that in her trial hour
Sincerest proofs were given of all thy loving power,
At Bayeux and at Rome
Showing her Heaven as home!
Remember thou!

Remember that the Holy Father's hand
Within the Vatican was laid on thee.
The mystery, then, thou couldst not understand,
The mystic sign of suffering to be.

But now thy children here to thee uplift their prayer;
They bless thy bitter cross, that won thy coronet rare.
Upon thy brow,- fair sight! -
There shine, in Heaven's own light,
Nine lilies brightl

    August, 1894.

WHAT I USED TO LOVE.

COMPOSED AT THE REQUEST OF HER SISTER
CELINE, SOME MONTHS AFTER THE LATTER'S ENTRANCE INTO CARMEL.

"I have in my Beloved the mountains, the solitary and wooded valleys, the foreign islands, the resounding rivers, the murmur of the amorus zephyrs, the peaceful night, so like the dawn of day, the harmonious solitude, -all that charms and that augments love." -St. John of the Cross.

Oh, how I love your memory,
My childhood days, so glad and free!
To keep my innocence, dear Lord, for Thee,
Thy love came to me night and day,
Alway.

So, when a little child was I,
To Thee I gave me utterly
Making with joy to Thee my promise high,
To wed a King beyond my view,--
Jesu!

I loved the Mother loved by Thee;
Saint Joseph, too, was friend to me.
How near Thy promised heaven seemed to be,
When shone, reflected in mine eyes,
The skies!

I loved the fields of wheat, the plain
Of emerald grass, the gentle rain.
Joy grew so great in me, 'twas almost pain!

How dear my sisters' presence there;
How fair!
I loved to cull the grass, the flowers,
Forget-me-nots in leafy bowers;
I found the violets' perfume, all the hours,--
With crocus growing neath my feet,
Most sweet.

I loved the daisies fair and white;
Our Sunday walks, - oh, what delight!
The azure skies so gloriously bright;
The birds that sang upon the tree
For me!
I loved my little shoe to grace,
Each Christmas in the chimney place;
To find it there at morn, how swift I'd race!
The feast of heaven, I hailed it well;
Noel!

I loved my mother's gentle smile,
Her thoughtful glance that said, the while:
"Eternity doth me from you beguile.
I go to heaven, my God, to be
With Thee!

"I go to find, in realms above,
My angel band in Mary's love. ah, prove,
The children whom I leave below, ah, prove,
Jesu! to them their guide and stay,
Alway!

Oh, how I loved my heavenly Lord,
In His blest Sacrament adored!
He bound me to Him by His given word
That He my Spouse from infancy
Would be!

I loved, upon the terrace fair,
My father's reveries to share;
To feel his gentle kisses on my hair.

I loved that father who shall tell
How well!

Teresa, seated on his knee,
Listened with me there, tenderly,
To those melodious songs he sang for me.
Those accents sweet I can not yet
Forget.

O Memory, what joys you bring!
You wake the thought of many a thing
That flew from me, long since, like birds awing.
Faces I see, voices I hear
How dear!

At sunset's hour I loved to be,
Teresa, heart to heart with thee;
Thy soul was as my very own to me.
My sister friend, my love, wert thou
As now.

Hand clasped in hand our hymns we sang.
Above earth's noisy clash and clang,
Our voices through the holy twilight rang.
Our dreams were then to Carmel given,
And heaven.

In Switzerland and Italy
The fairest scenes were shown to me;
But fairer yet I deemed the sight to be
Of him, - Father of Christendom,
At Rome!

The Coliseum's hallowed ground,
With rapturous joy, my footsteps found;
The Catacombs re-echoed to the sound
Of hymns I sang to Thee, th' Adored,
My Lord !

What sorrows followed then, amain;

What fears have filled my heart with pain!
But Jesus came to help me, and sustain,
And His dear cross has been my stay
Alway.
I fled the world, I turned my face,
And, in a quiet resting place,
I sought in silent prayer for constant grace
My load to bear, and for my grief
Relief.

I loved to hear, from distant towers,
The sweet church bells ring out the hours;
I loved to cull, through burning tears, the flowers
And hear, at eve, among the trees,
The breeze.

I loved the swallows' graceful flight,
The turtledoves' low chant at night,
The pleasant sound of insects gay and bright,
The grassy vale where doth belong
Their song.

I loved the delicate morning dew,
On Bengal rose of charming hue;
I loved to see the virginal bee accrue
Its store of honey from the flower,--
Its dower.

I loved to gather autumn leaves;
And, where the moss a carpet weaves,
How oft, from 'mongst the vines, my hand receives
A butterfly, so light of wing,-
Fair thing!

I loved the glow worm on the sod;
The countless stars, so near to God!
But most I loved the beauteous moon, endowed
With shining disk of silver bright,
At night.

To my dear father, worn and old,
I gave myself with love untold.
He was all to me. Joy, and home, and gold,
Were mine in him; for him my kiss,
My bliss.

We loved the sweet sound of the sea,
The storm, the calm, all things that be,
At eve, the nightingale sang from the tree.
Oh, seemed to us like seraphim
Its hymn!

But came one day when his sweet eyes
Sought Jesus' cross with glad surprise...
And then - my precious, loving father dies!
His last dear glance to me was given;
Then- heaven!

Jesus, with hand benign and blest,
Took Celine's treasure to his rest,
Where endless joys are evermore possessed;
Placing him near his throne of love,
Above!

Now, Lord, I am Thy prisoner here;
Gone are the joys once held so dear.
I have found out,-- none last, all seek their bier.
I have seen all my joys pass by,
And die.

The grass is withered in its bed;
The flowers within my hands are dead.
Would that my weary feet, Jesu! might tread
Thy heavenly fields, and I might be
With Thee!

E'en as the thirsting hart doth crave
Its lips in some cool stream to lave,
I seek from Thee, Jesu! the healing wave.
I need, to calm my ardors and my fears,

Thy tears.

Thy love, naught else, attracts my soul;
Heaven is my only aim, my goal;
Love, Love divine, has me in Its control.
I seek the Lamb upon His throne,
Alone.

Jesu! Thou art that Lamb divine;
Naught else I crave, if I am Thine.
In Thee all things in heaven and earth are mine!
Thou art the lovely Flower of spring,
My King!

Thou art the Lily, pure and fair;
Thy perfume sweet embalms the air.
O Bunch of sacred Myrrh, divinely rare,
Upon my heart, I beg Thee, stay
Alway!

Thy love goes with me where I go!
In Thee have I the sparkling snow,
The rains, the lofty hills, the valleys low,
The babbling brooks, the leafy trees,
The breeze!

All these I have in Thee, dear Lord:
The yellow wheat, the harvest horde,
The Rose of Sharon,--type of Thee, Adored!
Round me what flowers of charming dyes
Arise!

I have the dear melodious lyre,
The solitude of my desire,
My waves, and mighty rocks, and brilliant fire,
My birds that sing, my murmuring stream,
- Fair dream!

My rainbow in my rain washed skies,
Horizon where my suns arise,

Island in far-off seas, pearl I most prize,
Springtime and butterflies, I see
In Thee!

Thy love is like the flowers of May,
The palm-trees where the breezes play,
The nights almost as bright and light as day.
In Thee I find what shall not cease,-
Sweet peace!

Delicious grapes in Thee are mine,
The purple burden of the vine;
The virgin forest and the stately pine,
The fair haired children, Lord, I see
With Thee!

In Thee I have the springs, the rills,
The mignonette, the daffodils,
The eglantine, the harebell on the hills,
The trembling poplar, sighing low
And slow.

In Thee I have the waving wheat,
The winds that murmur low and sweet.
All Mary's flowers, once blooming at my feet,
The glowing plain, the tender grass, I see
In Thee.

Beneath my habit's plain, coarse fold
Thou givest me rare gems and gold.
Within my clasp what brilliant rings I hold,- Pearls, sapphires, rubies, diamonds bright,--
Tonight.

The lovely lake, the valley fair
And lonely, in the lambent air,
The ocean touched with silver everywhere,
In Thee their treasures, all combined,
I find.

I have the barque on mighty seas,
Its shining track, the shore, the breeze,
The sun that sinks behind the leafy trees,
Lighting the clouds, ere it expire,
With fire.

In Thee, the glorious stars are mine;
And often at the day's decline
I see, as through some veil silken and fine,
Beckoning from heaven, our fatherland,
Thy hand!

O Thou Who governest all the earth,
Who giv'st the mighty forests birth,
And at one glance mak'st all their life of worth!
On me Thou gazest, from above,
With love.

I have Thy Face, I have Thy Heart!
Lo! I am wounded with thy dart;
Thou dost Thy sacred kiss to me impart.
I love Thee! Thee alone I view,
Jesu!

I go, to chant, with angel throngs,
The homage that to Thee belongs.
Soon let me fly away, to join their songs!
Oh, let me die of love, I pray,
One day!

Drawn by the light, the insect flies
To meet the flame wherein it dies.
So, to Thy light, my longing soul would rise;
So would I gladly in that tire,
Expire!

I hear, e'en I, Thy last and least,
The music from Thy heavenly feast;
There, there, receive me as Thy loving guest!
There, to my harp, oh, bid me sing,

My King!

Mary I go to see, and there
The saints, and those once treasured here.
Life is all past, and dried at last each tear.
To me my home again is given,
In heaven!

        April 28, 1895.

Fifth Part

SPIRITUAL RECREATIONS
JESUS AT BETHANY

MARY MAGDALENE.
My God, Thy work complete!
At last I seek Thy grace.
Here at Thy holy feet,
Today I choose my place.
From earth I sought in vain
For ease, or joy, or rest;
Sorrow and weary pain
Alone have filled my breast.

OUR LORD.
Yes, Magdalene, rest here,
With contrite, humble heart.
Men's scorn no longer fear!
Choose thou the better part.
Hereafter live in peace,
Holy and pure, for Me;
And I shall never cease
To suffer, child, for thee.

MARY MAGDALENE.
It is too much! My sore
And burdened heart will break.
Could I be born once more,
Or die, for Thy sweet sake!
But I have caused Thy grief,
For me Thou art to die.
How shall I find relief
For all this misery?

OUR LORD.
Yes, many, many tears
Mine eyes have shed for thee
Yet speedily thy fears
Shall change to love for Me.

Thy soul, made pure again,
By one calm word of Mine,
In heaven, free from pain
Shall live a life divine.

MARY MAGDALENE.
Holy and stainless One!
How dare I seek Thy face?
What have I ever done
To win from Thee such grace?
I spurned in other years
Thy patient love for me;
Now, naught have I but tears
To offer Lord, to Thee.

OUR LORD.
Those pure, repentant tears
Shine brighter in My sight
Than any star appears
In radiant glow at night.
Than precious pearls more dear
Thy contrite heart today. O sorrowing soul, draw near!
Thy guilt is washed away.

MARY MAGDALENE
Thou Lord of heaven and earth,
What marvelous mystery!
Hath nothing, then, the worth
To win Thy heart from me?
Behold, how full of charms
The hill, and sea, and sky,
The lambs that seek Thine arms
The rivers flowing by!

OUR LORD.
I see the lilies bloom,
Unsullied, fair, and white;
Yet My large heart hath room
For thy heart's rose tonight.
That rose at last has won

My choice 'mid flowerets rare
From all beneath the sun
I choose its blossoms fair.

MARY MAGDALENE.
The bird's pure, warbling voice
Chants sweetest song to Thee;
The rippling brooks rejoice,
And praise Thee merrily;
The lily of the vale
Its perfumes hastes to bring
And petals, starlike, pale,
Before Thy feet to fling.

OUR LORD.
On ivoried, regal throne,
In glorious array,
The great King Solomon
Is less than these today;
The daisies in the field
Surpass his princely state;
And yet to thee they yield,
On thee they gladly wait!

MARY MAGDALENE.
A virginal train above,
With robes more white than snow,
Give thee their constant love,
And go where Thou dost go.
I, of a blighted life,
Offer the end to Thee,
From its frail morning rife
With bitter misery.

OUR LORD
I love the fires of dawn,
So bright, so pure, so fair;
But ah! I also love
The radiant evening air.
The soul, if it repent,

Shall find at last its home,
There where the sinless tent,
'Neath heaven's o'erspreading dome.

MARY MAGDALENE.
The angels there delight
To show their love for Thee.
Upon their phalanx white
Thy blessing ever be!
A sinful soul am I,
Who naught have merited.
Must Thou not pass me by?
Is mine the children's bread?

OUR LORD.
Higher than angels mount,
Shalt thou ascend one day!
Close, close to Love's own fount,
Shalt thou abide alway!
But first, on earth a while
In prayer live silently,
And thus gain souls from guile
To give their hearts to Me.

MARY MAGDALENE.
Oh! with what ardent zeal
My heart at last doth burn!
What deep desire I feel
To give Thy love return!
Yet souls to win for Thee,
Too weak, too blind, am I.
Lend Thou Thy heart to me;-
None then shall pass me by.

MARTHA.
Lord, one word I ask! Behold my sister there!
Now bid her, dearest Lord, to help me serve Thy meal.
She thinks not of my tasks; for me she hath no care;
She ought to wait on Thee; for me some pity feel!

OUR LORD.
Dear Martha, hostess kind and good!
Why should you thus your sister blame?
True, naught she thinks about My food,
Yet waits she on Me all the same.

MARTHA.
Ah, Lord divine and dear! 'tis this surprises me.
Ought she not, then, awhile, to cease to dream and pray?
Should she not choose what gift shall be her gift to Thee,
Who lavishly dost give to her and me each day?

OUR LORD.
Nay, Martha! listen to My Word!
Your faithful, generous love I know;
Yet doth your sister to her Lord
As faithful love and homage show,

MARTHA.
Deep myst'ries are these words that greet mine ears today.
I can not help but think,- oh! let me tell my thought!
Better to work good works than many prayers to say;-
The love I feel for Thee must into deeds be wrought.

OUR LORD.
True, Martha! works are needful here;
I came, Myself, to work with care;
Yet I would have this truth stand clear;
One must transfigure work with prayer.

MARTHA.
I knew that I was right; for, did I idly rest,
No charm should I possess in Thy benignant eyes;
So I made haste, to serve for Thee, my holy Guest,
Some pleasant food, to win Thy praise;- 'tis all I prize.

OUR LORD.
Generous your ardent soul, and good!
Martha, your works show forth your worth;
Yet would you know the only food

That I desire to have on earth?
One single work is needful here!
Your sister, biding near My heart,
In love's own prayer, divinely dear,
Hath chosen thus the better part.
Yes, this the part that is the best!
So I declare, and Truth am I.
Now, Martha, come and share her rest,
Her blessed rest, for Love am I!

MARTHA.
At last I understand! O Jesus, Love supreme,
Thy glance hath pierced my soul, Thy meaning now I see.
My gifts are all too small, my services a dream;
My heart the priceless gift that Thou wouldst have from me.

OUR LORD.
Yes, 'tis thy loving heart I crave;
For this I came from heaven above.
The glories 'tis My right to have,
I left, to seek your love, your love!

MARTHA.
Why, then, O Saviour dear, if I may ask Thee this,
Why, within Simon's house, didst greatly praise Marie?
For surely in her life she gave Thee pain, I wis;
And stormy days, in her, Thy sorrowing eyes must see

OUR LORD.
Martha! I understand her heart,
By pain and sin and sorrow rent;
For souls love much if pardoned much,
And sorely, sorely they repent.

MARTHA.
Amazed am I the more by Thy great love and power,
For naught know I, dear Lord, of sin's wild strength and shame.
What do I owe Thee, then Who, from my earliest hour,
Hast shielded me in peace, and kept me free from blame?

OUR LORD.
A soul kept pure through all its days,--
Chief masterpiece of Love Divine,-
Should give Me rapturous, endless praise,
And wholly and alone be Mine.
Yes, Martha, you have charmed My sight,
By lifelong, stainless purity;
Yet, while your soul is spotless white,
Your sister hath humility

MARTHA.
To win Thy love, dear Lord! through all my life to be,
Earth's honors I will scorn, and all its pomps despise,
And Mary's part will choose, while working still for Thee;
Thy love alone shall be of value in mine eyes.

OUR LORD.
Many the souls you thus shall claim
From sin's dark haunts to seek My Face;
And you shall bear afar the flame
Of faith, and love's immortal grace.

MARTHA AND MARY.
Thy voice, O Jesus Christ! is sweetest melody,
That wins our love to Thee, and sets our hearts on fire.
Abide Thou here alway, our Life on earth to be:
Abide Thou here alway, our hearts' supreme Desire!

OUR LORD.
True joy have I at Bethany,
Where find I oft a welcome true;
And in my Father's home shall be
A wondrous blessing granted you.

Yes, you the mystery comprehond
That makes drear earth My precious prize;
For souls of prayer are dear to Me,
A vast reward for sacrifice.

Beyond heaven's joys I prize such souls!

Heaven's glories, one day, yours shall be;
My goods your loving prayer controls,
Your Spouse am I eternally.

Here, faithful friends, ye gave Me meat;
But, in the feast at heaven's board,
Ye shall sit down to food more sweet,
While on you waits your God and Lord.

    July 29, 1895

BIRDCAGE OF THE INFANT JESUS

For us, poor exiles from our birth,
God made the pretty little birds;
Among the hills and dales of earth
They sing His praises without words;
But sometimes playful childish hands,
Choosing the ones they like the best,
Keep them in cages, where the bands
Are gilded bars for these oppressed.

O Jesus, little Brother dear!
For us from Heaven didst Thou flee;
Thou knowest well Thy bird cage here
Is Carmel, and Thy birds are we.

Our cage is gilded not at all,
Yet oh! how precious 'tis to me!
To hill or plain from its high wail
Not one of us would wish to flee.
Let not the outer world intrude!
No joy to us it now could bring.
Child Jesus! in our solitude
For Thee, for Thee alone, we sing.
Thy tiny hand has us beguiled;
Thy infant charms no words can tell;
Thy smile, most sweet and Holy Child!
Has won Thy birds to love Thee well.

Here finds the simple, candid soul
The only object of its love;
Here is the vulture's fierce control
No longer dreaded by the dove.

Upon the wings of burning prayer
The ardent heart ascends on high,
As swift the lark doth cleave the air,
With sweet, enraptured, joyful cry.
Here, in Thy praises to engage,
The nightingale and veery came.
O Little Jesus! in Thy cage
Thy birds are carolling Thy Name.

The little bird it always sings,
Nor fear for its small meal doth know;
A grain of wheat contentment brings;
It sows not, spins not, here below.
Within this cage where we have fled,
Is all provided through Thy care;
The one thing needful, Thou hast said,
Is just to love Thee, Child most fair!
So, through the hours, we sing Thy praise,
With glad, pure spirits ever blest.
We know the angels, all the days,
Love Carmel's birds within their nest.

Jesu! Thy bitter tears to dry,
That sinful men have wrung from Thee,
Thy birds to win back souls will try,
By their sweet songs of ecstasy.
One day, when earth and time are o'er,
And Thy clear call to us is given,
Then angel-hands shall ope the door;
Thy birds shall take their flight to Heaven;
And there, with charming, songful hosts
Of little cherubs glad and gay,
Thy happy birds from Carmel's coasts
Shall praise Thy Holy Name alway.
   December 25, 1896.

THE FLIGHT OF THE HOLY FAMILY INTO EGYPT

A Fragment.
THE ANGEL WARNS ST. JOSEPH.

All swiftly, silently,
To Egypt take your flight!
Depart, this very night!

Herod his fury now,
Is even to madness heaping;
He longs to slay the Lamb
In Mary's tendance sleeping,
Take Mother and Child, and go
From an impending woe.

SONG OF THE ANGELS ACCOMPANYING
THE HOLY FAMILY.

Wonders on wonders piled!
Jesus, of Heaven the Lord,
Now upon earth exiled,
Flee, from a mortal's sword.
So, unto God in flight,
Oh, let us give our love;
Let our white wings tonight
Protect Him from above!
Now bring the flowers most fair
To strew before His way!
A lullaby prepare,
Of songs most sweet and gay!

Console His Mother's heart
By singing of His charms.
How fair, how sweet, Thou art,
Reposing in her arms

Oh, let us speed afar,
For here dire perils are!
Fly, on this very night,

From dangers and from fright!
The Virgin bears our Star,
Beneath her veil afar,
The Star of the elect,
Whom longing hearts expect.

Behold! Heaven's Lord
Flees from a mortal's sword!

THE ANGEL OF THE DESERT.

I come, I come, to sing your charms divine,
Blest Family who lure me to this place.
In this drear desert, lo! to-night doth shine
A Star more fair than heaven in all its grace.
But who shall comprehend this mystery:-
He came unto His own -they bade Him go!
A wanderer on the earth He made is He,
And none discern His beauty here below.
But if the great Thine empire now despise,
Thou King of Heaven, Thou mystic promised Star!
Long for Thy reign have looked. the teardimmed eyes,
And long the unhappy sought Thee from afar.
O Word Eternal! Wisdom true and deep!
Thy gifts are here, but they are for the meek:
The childlike soul, the tried, and them who weep,
It is to them, one day, Thy voice shall speak.

For Thou Thy wisdom often dost impart
To ignorant men, if they but humble be;
And Thou dost call the sinful to Thy Heart,
Because in them Thine image Thou dost see.
A day shall come, when, in the selfsame fold,
The lamb beside the lion safe shall feed;
And in Thy refuge here, this desert old,
Thy Name shall call forth many a holy deed.

O hidden God! what virginal souls, one day,
Catching from Thy vast fire of love the flame,
Shall hither haste, where Thou hast led the way;

And all these wastes for their possession claim.
Their ardent souls, their love like seraphs blest,
Shall fill the angels with supreme delight;
And hell shall tremble at their hymns, addrest
Unto God's greater glory, day and night

Then Satan shall, in frantic jealousy,
Seek to deplete these houses of our Lord;
But knows he not the power and majesty
Of this frail Child, humble, unknown, ignored.
He dreams not that a lowly virgin heart
Forever dwells in safety and in peace;
He dreams not of the strength, beyond his art,
She has from God, whose wonders never cease.

It may be that, one day, Thy spouses dear
Must share Thy exile, O Thou Holy Child!
But none shall quench their love, that burns most clear
Despite their exile and men's fury wild.
Nor shall the vile world's sacrilegious spite
Turn from their goal the virgins of the Lord;
Nor ever soil their robes of spotless white,
Nor mar their likeness to their King adored.

Ungrateful world! thy reign is well nigh done
Dost thou not see how this most holy Child
Culls joyously these roses like the sun,
These martyrs' palms, these lilies undefiled?
Dost thou not see His faithful virgin band,
Holding their burning lamps with love alight
Dost thou not see heaven's portals open stand
The saints to welcome in, to glory bright?

O happy moment! joy that knows no shade!
When the elect in gladness enter there;
And for their love, the great reward is paid,-
To see God's face, that promised Vision fair!
Life's exile o'er, gone are all pain and woe;
E'en faith itself, and hope itself, shall cease;
But everlasting rest those souls shall know.

The ecstasy of love and endless peace.

January 21, 1896.

THE LITTLE DIVINE BEGGAR OF CHRISTMAS

An angel appears, bearing the Child Jesus in
his arms; and he sings as follows:

Sisters! I bring to you the Adored,
The Eternal God, so small, so weak;
I plead for the Incarnate Word,
Because as yet He cannot speak.
To Jesus, exiled from His home,
The cruel world no shelter grants;
And so to Carmel's shade I come,
To find the shelter that He wants.

Ever your praise, your tenderness,
Your welcome sweet, your warm caress,
Be for this Child!
Oh, burn with love, for He loves you,
This Child, who is your God and Lord.
Pathetic mystery! He who begs, tonight, of you,
Is the Eternal Word!
Come then, my Sisters! without fear,
Each in her turn, to Jesus' feet,
Offering your love to Him most dear,
And you shall know His will so sweet,
Yes, I will tell you the desires
Of Jesus born amid the snow;
For you are pure as angels are,
And you can suffer too, you know!

Ever your cares, your suffering,
And all your joys so light of wing,
Be for this Child!
Oh, burn with love, for He loves you,
This Babe, who is your God and Lord!
Pathetic mystery! He who begs, tonight, of you,

Is the Eternal Word!

The angel, having placed the Child Jesus inthe crib, offers to the Mother prioress, and then to all the Carmelites, a basket of little notes or envelopes. Each takes one, haphazard, and without opening it gives it to the angel, who then sings the petition therein contained, -- the gift which the Divine Child asks from each in turn.

I.-1 A GOLD THRONE

Jesus, Christ, your only treasure,
Asks one special gift of you.
No gold throne was in the stable,
Yet such treasure is His due.
Sinners' souls are like the stable,
Bare and cold in winter's snow,
Off'ring to Him no soft shelter,
No bright fire's cheerful glow.
Souls of sinners, save them, Sister!
That the throne our Lord desires;
Seeks He, too, the royal welcome
Of your pure heart's holy fires.

I.-2 SOME MILK.

He Who feeds the souls predestined
With His Essence all Divine,
Makes Himself the Infant Jesus
To be your delight, and mine.
Up in heaven His joy is perfect;
Here below, a beggar He

Quickly fetch some milk, dear Sister;
Baby Jesus thirsts, you see.
Ah! our little Brother Jesus
Smiles on you. Noel! Noel!
Down from heaven to earth He cometh
In your childlike heart to dwell.

I.-3 SOME LITTLE BIRDS

You, dearest Sister! long to know
What you can do for Jesus' sake,
So joyfully I haste to tell
How you His glorious smiles can wake.
Go, catch for Him some charming birds,
And in the stable let them sing,
For they are types of children's souls,
So dear to this Child Christ their King.
Their pretty hymns, their baby prayers,
His sleep like joy bells gently break.
Pray for them then; in heaven one day
Those children's souls your crown will make.

I.-4 A STAR.

Sometimes, when all the skies are black
With gloomy clouds, and no stars shine,
Our little Jesus grieves alone,-
He craves your love, yes, yours and mine.
Then give to Him the light He wants,
Be like a bright and shining star;
And let your virtues, like a lamp,
Shed welcoming radiance near and far.
So may your rays lead souls to heaven,
The sinful souls for whom He died.
This Child Divine, our Morning Star,
Asks you to be His star, His bride.

I.-5 A LYRE

MY little Sister,'waiting there,
Your gift for Bethlehem's Babe to hear,
Your heart for His melodious lyre
Is what He asks in accents clear.
In heaven's high court swells up alway
The angels' song with incense sweet;
And yet He loves, in Carmel's shade,
To hear your praises at His feet.
So, dearest Sister! 'tis your heart,

Whose melodies our Lord desires.
By night, by day, consume away,
With songs of love, in love's sweet fires.

I.-6 SOME ROSES.

Your soul, dear, is a lily sweet,-
Jesus and Mary love it well.
Hear what the heavenly Bridegroom speaks Softly, yet clear as altar bell; -
Ah! if I love the lily white,
Symbol of innocence like snow,
Yet for the rose of penitence
I also feel My heart aglow.
Let your warm tears for sinners fall,-
What joy your love will give Me then!
So can I gather at My Will
Those roses dear, the hearts of men.

I.-7 A VALLEY.

As by the shining of the sun
Nature is glorified and gay;
As by its radiance field and vale
Grow fair and strong and green alway;

So doth our Jesus, Son divine,
Approach you with His sweet caress,
Shining at His own matin hour,
Your loving heart to heal and bless.
Lo! He is born on Christmas morn,
Your exiled soul to find and cheer,
To fill your days with His warm rays:
So be His smiling valley, dear!

I.-8 SOME REAPERS.

Lo! here on earth, 'neath other skies,
In spite of storm and winter's snow
Already our dear Little One
Hath found some harvests here below.

But, ah! to gather them He needs
Reapers on fire with quenchless love,
And glad to suffer or to die
For Him who reigns in Heaven above
Noel Noel to Carmel's shade
I come, because His will is thine.
Sister! form apostolic souls,
To reap the harvest fields divine.

The following was the stanza that was drawn by Sister Teresa of the Infant Jesus herself. Only three months later she heard the first call of the Divine Master invite her to leave earth for heaven.

I.-9 A BUNCH OF GRAPES

I want some sweet and cooling fruit,
A bunch of grapes so smooth and fair,
To moisten the small, thirsting lips
Of this dear Babe within my care.
Your lot, my Sister! oh, how blest,
For those choice grapes He asks of you,
Within His vineyard to be prest!
The hearts of all men are His due.
His tiny hand like snow-flake white
Upon your throbbing heart shall lie,
And from all touch of earth's delight
Absorb it into His on high.

I.-10 A LITTLE WHITE HOST.

Oh! we how with each morning's light
Jesus, the Child divinely fair,
Into a little snow white host
Transforms Himself, that you may share
His life; and yet with greater love,
He longs to change you into Him.
Your heart His precious treasure is,
His happiness, His joy supreme.
Noel! Noel! from heaven He comes,
To fill your soul with glorious light;

The Lamb of God to you descends,
Now be His pure white host tonight!

II-1 A SMILE.

Ah! the wicked world despises
Love that Jesus feels for men;
And His heavenly eyes are moistened
With hot bitter tears for them;
And His little arms He stretches,
Dearest Sister, unto you.
Shall I tell you what the comfort
That I think He seems to sue?
See! His look is asking of you,
And His sweet eyes seem to say:
Smile on all! That smile suffices
To wipe all My tears away.

II.-2 SOME PLAYTHINGS.

Would you like to be the plaything
Of this Child so fair and sweet?
Would you, dear one! like to please Him?
Then lie humbly at His feet.
If He chooses to caress you,
If He lifts you to His breast,
Yes, if He seems tired of you,
Count yourself among the blest.
Be His happy Christmas plaything,
Seeking just to do His will;
And in heaven with countless blessings
He, your happy heart, will fill.

II.-3 A PILLOW.

Oft I see the Baby Jesus
Wakeful in His manger bed.
Would you know the reason? Dear ones,
There's no pillow for His head.
Ah! I know your ardent longing

To console Him night and day.
Give your heart to be His pillow,
That is what He wants alway;
And be ever meek and humble,
Then you will be greatly blest.
You will hear Him softly saying:
In your heart how sweet My rest!

II.-4 A FLOWER.

All the earth with snow is covered,
Everywhere the white frosts reign;
Winter and his gloomy courtiers
Hold their court on earth again.
But for you has bloomed the Flower
Of the fields, Who comes to earth
From the fatherland of heaven,
Where eternal spring has birth.
Near the Rose of Christmas, Sister!
In the lowly grasses hide,
And be like the humble flowerets,-
Of heaven's King the lowly bride!

II.-5 SOME BREAD.

Day by day, at morn and even,
Still the holy words are said:
O our Father up in Heaven!
Give to us our daily bread,
Yet your God, become your Brother,
Suffers hunger as you do;
And His childish voice is asking
For a little bread from you.
Ah! my Sister! Jesus wishes
Just your love,- how great your bliss!
Let your soul be pure and spotless,
For His daily bread is this.

II.-6 A MIRROR.

Children like to have you place them,
Near a mirror clear and fair;
Then they greet with childish rapture
The bright face that they see there.
Come, then, to the favored stable,
Let your soul like crystal glow.
Let the Word, become an Infant,
In your heart His likeness know!
Sister, be the living image,
Of your Spouse,- His mirror clear;
All the beauty of your Jesus
He would have in you appear.

II.-7 A PALACE.

The great and noble of the earth,
In palaces they proudly dwell;
The poor and lonely find their home
In hut, in cabin, and in cell.
So in a humble cattle shed
The Christ Child lies, this Christmas night;
Leaving His palace in the skies,
He veils His glory's dazzling light.
Your heart loves poverty, I know;
You count yourself divinely blest;
So Jesus finds a palace home
Within your humble, happy breast.

II.-8 A CROWN OF LILIES.

Sinners will crown with thorns, one day
The holy, heavenly head of Christ.
What pains and sorrows will be His,
To gain us graces all unpriced.
Now may your virginal sweet soul
Make Him tonight His woes forget;
And for His royal lily crown
Your Sisters' souls before Him set!

Draw very near to Jesus' throne,
To charm His lovely tear dimmed eyes;
Make of these virgin souls His crown
Of snow white lilies beyond price!

III.-1 SOME BONBONS.

Sister dear, the little ones
Like so much the sweet bonbons!
Bring some then, and quickly fill
Jesus' small white hand tonight!
By His smile He doth invite
You to do His childish will.
This wee King, so frail, so weak,
Carmel's candies He doth seek; -
What they are, you surely guess!
Give Him your austerity
And your holy poverty,
He your gift will quickly bless.

III.-2 A CARESS.
Little Jesus, dear, from you
Nothing more doth softly sue
Than a very sweet caress.
Give Him all your love today,
And your gift He will repay;
With His love your soul will bless.

If a Sister weep tonight,
Sore at heart where all are bright,
Ah! at once, with tenderness,
Beg the little Holy Child
That His small hand undefiled
Dry her tears with its caress.

III.-3 A CRADLE.

Many hearts God's favors want,
Would have Jesus always grant
Gifts and presents without end.

If He seem awhile to sleep,
Few their watch beside Him keep;
Few remain His faithful friend.

Get Him sleep that none may break;
Though we know His Heart doth wake;
Even in dreams our Jesus weeps.
So His cradle, Sister, be!
Guard the sweet Lamb tenderly,
Smiling on Him while He sleeps.

III-4 SOME LINENS.

See the dear Child's tiny hand
Point - to make you understand -
At the rough and rasping straw.
Won't you grant His wish tonight,
And bring linens pure and white,
O'er His manger bed to draw?

Make excuses kind and true,
Whatsoe'er your Sisters do,
Loving all for Christ their King.
Thus your ardent charity,
And your true simplicity,
Are the linens you can bring.

III.-5 SOME FIRE.

Our sweet Jesus, Fire of love,
Light and Warmth of heaven above,
In the stable, cold is He!
Yet, in the far, shining sky,
Angels, living flames on high,
Wait on Him in ecstasy.

Here on earth 'tis you must light
Blazing fires of love tonight,
In your heart, all free from sin;
Little shivering Jesus warm
In the shelter of your arm,

By the souls your prayers shall win!

III.-6 A CAKE.

Well we know that children small
Eagerly for cakes will call!
This dear Child will not disdain
Even such a gift tonight!
Offer it with great delight;
You His happy smile will gain.

Know you what to this Child King
Real content will surely bring?
'Tis obedience prompt and true.
As He bowed to Mary's will,
So do you the rule fulfil,
Such the cake He asks of you.

III.-7 SOME HONEY.

In the pretty floweret's cup,
When the morning sun comes up,
You can see the tiny bee,
Flitting fast through summer hours,
Visiting the woodland bowers,
Gathering honey steadily.

Ah! of love your treasure make;
And, each day, for Christ's dear sake,
To His holy cradle come.
All the honey of your love
Give, sweet bee! to this meek Dove;
Make His Heart your hive and home!

III-8. A LAMB.

Would you charm the Lamb of God?
In the path that He hath trod
Tread today with willing feet!
Leaving all things here below,

Seek alone His will to know;
Do His will surpassing sweet!

O my Sister! be His own;
Seek for naught but God alone!
He will give you perfect rest.
Mary, leaning o'er His bed,
Will see another childish head,
Close to His, and oh! how blest.

The Angel, taking again the Child Jesus in his arms, sings what follows:

The dear Child Jesus thanks you all,
For all your gifts, this Christmas night;
And all your names His tiny hand
Within His book of life will write.
Since in this Carmel He hath found
Such joy and peace,
Rewards in heaven He'll store for you,
That shall not cease.
And if you ever faithful are
To all the vows you make tonight,
Then love will give you wings to fly
Unto a far sublimer height.

Your exile o'er,
Jesus and Mary you shall see
Forevermore!

THE ANGELS OF THE CRIB.

FRAGMENT.

THE ANGEL OF THE CHILD JESUS.

Thou Word of God, Thou Glory of God!
In awe I gazed on Thee above;
And now I see that Glory of God,
That Word of God, made Man through love.
O Child, whose light doth blind the sight

Of angels in high heaven divine!
Thou'rt come to save the world tonight,
And who can fathom that love of Thine?
In swaddling bands
The Child God fies.
Lord of all lands!
Trembling before Thy face I veil mine eyes.

Yes, who can fathom this marvellous thing?
God makes Himself a little Child,
He, the eternal, almighty King,
Afar from His own heaven exiled!
Fain would I give Thee love for love!
Thee will I guard by day and night,
My utter fealty to prove,
Thou tiny Jesu, Light of Light!
Thy cradle so dear
Draws angels anear.
O Child God! now
Trembling before that humble crib I bow.

While earth has power from heaven to bring
My King to want and cold and woe,
Heaven holds no longer anything
To keep me from that world below.
My wings shall shield Thy Baby head;
Thee will I follow everywhere;
Beneath Thy tiny feet I'll fling
The sweetest flowers and most fair.

Oh, would some radiant star might fall,
To form Thy cradle, Baby bright!
Would I the dazzling snow could call,
To be Thy curtains pure and white!
Would all the lofty hills might bow
In lowly homage at Thy feet!
Oh, would the fields might bloom for Thee,
Celestial blossoms heavenly sweet!

For all the flowers are smiles of God,

Are distant echoes from His throne,
Are notes that wander far abroad
From that great harp He holds alone.
Those notes of harmony divine
Relate His goodness unto men,
And in their melody combine
To tell His saving love again.
O that sweet melody,
Exquisite harmony,
Silence of flowers
Ye tell His greatness, His wonders, His powers!

Well know I, Jesu! that Thy friends,
Thy dearest friends, are living flowers.
Thou travellest to earth's farthest ends,
To cull them for heaven's fadeless bowers.

Souls are the flowers with beauty rife
That draw Thee from the heavens high;
Thy tiny hand first gave them life,
And Thou for them wilt gladly die.
Mystery ineffable!
Thou, Word adorable,
Surely shalt one day weep
When Thou the harvest of those flowers shalt reap.

THE ANGEL OF THE HOLY FACE.

Yes, from the morning of Thy days, dear Child!
Thy blessed Face is bathed in burning tears.
Those tears upon that Face all undefiled
Still shall flow on throughout Thy earthly years.
O Face divine!
So fair Thou art
From angel eyes
The glories of the skies depart.

Under its veil of anguish sore and dread,
I see Thy loveliness all charms above;
In Thy worn, pallid Face, O Jesu dead!

I see Thy Child face in its perfect love.

For pain to Thee, my Jesus! was so dear
That even Thy Baby eyes the future saw,
And Thou didst long to drink the chalice drear,
Thy very dreams could Thee to Calvary draw.
O wonderful dream!
Thou Child of a day,
From Thy face but one beam
Thrills my heart with its ray.

THE ANGEL OF THE RESURRECTION.

Angel of man's Redeemer! weep no more.
I come with comfort for sad hearts and sore.
This Child shall yet gain
All men's hearts as their King;
He shall arise and reign
Almighty, triumphing.

O God! concealed in childish guise before us,
I see Thee glorious,
O'er all things victorious.

I shall roll back the great tomb's rocky door,
I shall behold Thy lovely Face once more,
And I shall sing,
And I shall then rejoice,
When I shall see my King,
And hear again His voice,

Thy childish eyes, though dim tonight with tears,
Shall shine with heavenly light throughout the eternal years.
O Word of God!
Thy speech, like burning flame,
Shall sound one day abroad,
And all Thy love proclaim.

THE ANGEL OF THE EUCHARIST.

Gaze on, dear Angel, heavenward flown,
Gaze, while our King ascends on high;
But I, to seek His altar throne,
Down to the distant earth will fly.
Veiled in His Eucharist I see
The Almighty Lord, the Undefiled,
The Master of all things that be,
More tiny than the humblest child.

Here will I dwell in this blest piace,
The sanctuary of my King;
And here, before His veiled Face,
My hymns of ardent love will sing.
Here, to my heaven strung angel lyre,
My praise I'll chant, by night, by day,
To Him, the Feast for saint's desire,
To Him, the sinner's Hope and Stay.

Would that by miracle, I too
Could feed upon this heavenly Bread;
Could taste that Blood forever new,
That Blood which was for all men shed!
At least, with some pure longing soul,
I'll share my fires of love divine,br> That so, all fearless, glad and whole,
It may approach its Lord and mine.

THE ANGEL OF THE LAST JUDGMENT.

Soon shall the awful day of judgment come,
This wicked world shall feel the avenging flame;
All men shall hear pronounced their endless doom,
And these to bliss shall pass, and those to shame.
Then shall we see our God in glory bright,
No longer hidden in this cradle small;
Then shall we sing His triumph after fight,
And then proclaim Him Lord and King of all.

As stars shine out when furious storms are passed,
His eyes shall shine, now veiled in blood and tears;
And His eternal splendor shall at last

Appear again, after these anguished years.
Upon the clouds our Jesus shall be borne,
Beneath the standard of the cross on high;
And evil men who hailed Him once in scorn
Shall know their awful judge is drawing nigh.

Ah, ye shall tremble, habitants of earth!
Ah, ye shall tremble on that final day,
No longer able to withstand the wroth
Of this dear Child, the God of love today.
For you He chose to tread the path of pain,
Seeking your hearts alone, to Him so dear:
But when at last He comes to earth again,
How shall ye quail before His Face in fear!

ALL THE ANGELS, with the exception of THE ANGEL
OF THE LAST JUDGMENT.

O Jesu, deign to hear the prayer,
That we, Thy Angels offer Thee!
Thy people save, Thy people spare,
Thou who didst come the world to free!

With Thy small hand avert this dart,
Appease this Angel with the sword;
Save every meek and contrite heart
That seeks Thy mercy, dearest Lord!

THE CHILD JESUS.

My faithful Angels, tried and true!
Far from the heavenland of your birth,
Hear, for the first time, speak to you
The Eternal Word made Man on earth!

I love you well, O spirits pure!
Angels from heaven's high courts above!
Yet men I love with love as sure,
Yea, with an everlasting love.

I made their infinite desires,
Their souls were made at My decree;
A heart that kindles with My fires
Becomes a heaven on earth for Me.

The Angel of the Infant Jesus asks Him to gather upon earth an abundant harvest of innocent souls, before they have been tainted by the impure breath of sin.

ANSWER OF THE CHILD JESUS.

Dear Angel of My childhood's hours!
I grant the answer to thy prayer.
Many shall be the innocent flowers
I will preserve all lily fair.

Yes, I will cull those blossoms gay,
Fresh with their pure baptismal dew;
And they shall bloom in endless day,
In ecstasy forever new.

Their fair corollas, silvery bright,
More brilliant than a thousand fires,
Shall be the Milky Way of light
'Mid all the starry heavenly choirs.
I must have lilies for My crown,-
The Lily of the Field am I!
And I must have to grace my throne,
A sheaf of lilies in the sky.

The Angel of the Holy Face asks pardon for sinners.

ANSWER OF THE CHILD JESUS

Thou who dost gaze upon My Face
In ecstasy of seraph love,
Leaving for love of it thy place
Of glory in My heaven above!

Thy prayer I hear, I grant thy plea.

Each soul that on My name sahll call
Shall find relief, shall be set free
From Sin's dark curse, from Satan's thrall.

Thou who dost seek to honor here
My Cross, My Passion, My bruised Face:
Learn now this mystery, angel dear!
Each soul that suffers shares thy grace.

The radiance of its pain borne now,
In heaven upon thy face shall shine;
The martyr's halo decks thy brow,
His glory shall be drawn from thine.

The Angel of the Eucharist asks what he can do to console our Lord for the ingratitude of men.

ANSWER OF THE CHILD JESUS.

Dear Angel of the Eucharist!
Thou, thou dost charm Me every hour;
Thy song, by heaven's own breezes kissed,
Over My suffering soul hath power.

Ah, the great thirst of My desires!
I crave, I crave, the hearts of men.
Dear Angel, melt them with thy fires,
And win them to My Heart again!

Would each anointed priest might be
Like Seraphim beyond the skies,
What time he comes to offer Me
My pure and holy Sacrifice!

To work such miracle of grace,
It needs must be that night and day,
Souls near the attar seek a place
To watch and suffer, weep and pray.

The Angel of the Resurrection asks what will become of the poor exiled ones left on earth when the Saviour shall have ascended into heaven.

ANSWER OF THE CHILD JESUS.

Back to My Father I shall go,
Thither to draw the men I love;
And heaven's long bliss they then shall know,
When I shall welcome them above.

When the last hour of time appears,
My flock shall come again to Me;
And I shall be, for endless years,
Their Light, their Life, their Ecstasy

THE ANGEL OF THE LAST JUDGMENT.

Goodness supreme! and dost Thou then forget
Sinners must meet at last, the doom decreed ?
Dost Thou forget, in Thy great love, that yet,
Their number is nigh infinite indeed ?

At the last judgment I shall punish crime,
Evil before My wrath shall shrink and bow;
My sword is ready ... Jesu! 'tis the time.
My sword is ready to avenge Thee now.

THE CHILD JESUS

Great Angel, turn aside thy sword
I am the Messenger of Peace.
The nature taken by thy Lord
'Tis not thy work to judge. O cease!

'Tis I shall judge the human race,
Jesus My name, all names above.
I grant My elect ones boundless grace.
For men I died, and I am Love!

Dost thou not know that, every day,
The blasphemies of faithless lips

Before one love-glance pass away,
And find therein assured eclipse?

The souls I choose, the souls I spare,
Shall reign in glory like the sun.
'Tis Mine own life I give them there,
And they and I shall there be one.

THE ANGEL OF THE LAST JUDGMENT.

Before Thee, Child divine, the Cherubim bow lowly,
Lost in amaze as they Thy love all boundless see.
Fain would we die like Thee, on Calvary's summit holy,
Fain would we die like Thee!

REFRAIN.

Sung by all the Angels.

How great the bliss of man, Thy low and humble creature.
In ecstasy would fain each seraph undefiled
Put off, O Jesus sweet, his grand angelic nature,
Would fain become a child!

  Noel, 1894

POEMS IN HONOR OF JEANNE D'ARC

THE SHEPHERDESS OF DOMREMY HEARKENING TO HER VOICES.

Happy, happy am I,
Jeanne the shepherdess!
How swift my lambkins fly
To meet my kind caress.

How light my little crook;
How cool this verdant grove,
Beside whose babbling brook

In solitude I rove.

A lovely crown I weave
Of field flowers, fair and sweet;
What joy is mine to leave
That crown at Marv's feet!

Oh, how I love the flowers,
The birds, the rippling stream
The skies above these bowers
As fair as angel's dream.

The valleys and the rills
Rejoice my longing eyes;
The summits of the hills,
They seem to touch the skies!

But hark! What voices come
Upon the evening breeze?
Do angels seek my home
With melodies like these?

I question air and space,
I gaze into the skies;
And yet no slightest trace
Of angels greets my eyes.

Ah, past those clouds that bar
And veil them from my sight,
Would I might fly afar
To realms of radiant light!

ST. CATHERINE AND ST. MARGARET:

Thy pure sweet voice to heaven has pierced, dear child,
From this time forth committed to our care!
Thine angel guardian, ever undefiled,
Has borne to God on high thy earnest prayer.

Down from His heavenly palace we have flown,

From His high court on His eternal hill;
For by our voices He to thee makes known
His holy will.

Thou must go forth to save thy fatherland,
To guard the faith, uphold God's honor here.
Thou as a conqueror in His sight shall stand,
Preserved by Him and His own Mother dear.

(TO JEANNE, WHO WEEPS.)

Oh, dry thy tears, take comfort, tender heart!
Beyond these clouds gaze into heaven's delight;
In our ecstatic chants thou shalt have part,
Who by God's grace shalt conquer in the fight.

These sweet refrains thy soul shall fortify
Against approaching combat fierce and dire.
Jeanne! thou must suffer. Seek, then, from on high
A love like fire!

For the pure soul, in time's long dreary night,
Its only glory is, Christ's cross to bear;
And, in heaven's endless day, with splendor bright
That cross shall shine all radiant and fair.

ST. MICHAEL:

Michael am I, the guardian of France,
Great Captain of the armies of the skies;
Against hell's troops I march with sword and lance,
And the old serpent glares with curious eyes.
Once Satan far above the starry world
Desired to reign, higher than seraphs trod;
But, like a thunderbolt, at him I hurled
These words: " Oh, who is like to God!

At that same moment vengeance, dread, divine,
Oped hell's abyss and thither thrust him deep.
For that proud fallen angel, ah! no mercies shine;

For him, what eyes shall weep?

Pride tore down Satan from his lofty place,
And of that morning star an outcast made;
But when man, too, had trifled with God's grace,
Pity and comfort were to him displayed.
The Eternal Word, the Father's Equal Son,
Clothing Himself with poor humanity,
Back to His Father's heart the exiles won
By His profound humility.

Now that same Saviour deigns to succor France
But not by any mighty soldier's hand.
He hath cast down the proud; He gives the conquering lance
Unto a child's frail hand.

Jeanne! God has chosen thee His work to do.
Thou must depart, obedient to His call;
Unto thy fields, thy flocks, must bid adieu,
To this dear vale, these woods, thy home, thy all.
Be strong, go forth and save thy fatherland!
Go forth - fear naught; all danger now despise!
Go! in my might beside thee I shall stand.
See how the foe before thee flies!

Take thou this sword and bear it to the fray; -
Long hath God kept it for thy hand to bring.
Take for thy standard, child! this pure white flag today;
Then go,- and find the king!

JEANNE ALONE:

For Thee alone, O God, I quit my father's side,
I leave my cherished friends, my parish church so dear,
For Thee I leave my flocks, my valleys green and wide,
My peaceful home, - to fight. Forgive me, if I fear!
Instead of my white lambs, I must lead armed men;
To Thee I sacrifice my joy, my eighteen years.
I shall not see, alas! these flowery fields again;
To serve Thee, Lord, I go, 'mid shields and swords and spears.

My voice, that mingles now with the soft breezes' breath,
Shall soon resound amid war's clamors wild and drear;

The piercing, frightful cries of battle and of death,
Instead of sweet church bells, shall reach my straining ear.
Yet, I desire the cross; the sacrifice is light;
To suffer for Thee, Lord, ready and glad am I.
Now deign to call Thy child to this sublime delight!
Jesus, my Love, my All, for Thee I long to die.

ST. MICHAEL:

Thou must depart, O Jeanne! the time has come.
It is the Lord Who arms thee for the fray.
Soon shalt thou see our blest, eternal home!
Daughter of God! fear not to die today.

ST. MARGARET:

Thou, child, with Him shalt reign above.

ST. CATHERINE:

Wherever goes the Lamb, thy virgin soul shall go.
THE TWO SAINTS TOGETHER:

Like us, thou, too, shalt sing the love
And power of God most high, where crystal streamlets flow.

ST. MICHAEL:

Thy name, O Jeanne! on heaven's scroll is placed,
With all who died that France might live for aye;
There shall thy brow with glory's crown be graced,
Like royal queen upon her nuptial day.

THE SAINTS, offering to Jeanne the palm and crown:

With joy our loving eyes can see
The radiance that even now upon thy head streams down;

And from high heaven we bring to thee

ST. CATHERINE:

The martyr's glorious palm,

ST. MARGARET:

The martyr's crown.

ST MICHAEL, presenting the sword:

Before the victory must come the fight,
Not yet the crown, not yet the palm can be.
Win them where honor doth defend the right.
Jeanne! dost thou hear the bugle call to thee?

THE SAINTS TOGETHER:

Thee will we guard throughout the fray;
And splendid victories shall thy banner grace.
On thy pure brow, one happy day,
Our hand the glorious aureole shall place.

JEANNE, ALONE:

With you, dear saints, no foe I fear;
Upon the Lord of hosts I wait.
What time the battle draweth near,
His arm shall send deliverance great.

Oh, how I love my fatherland,
France, oldest daughter of the cross;
That love to sacrifice is fanned;
For her I count as gain all loss.

Ah, no! I fear not now to die,
Who long, dear God, Thy Face to see;
Yet, as I go, oh ! hear my cry:
Comfort my mother tenderly!

And thou, St. Michael, strengthen me.

ST. MICHAEL:

Hark! for already all the elect in heaven
Raise high their joyous chant, because they hear
The illustrious name of Martyr gladly given,
By Rome's great Pontiff, to this maiden dear.

I hear the universe declare
The virtues of this maid in warlike armor drest;
I hear God grant to her the rare
And grand and glorious title, Jeanne the Blest.

In those great days sore suff'ring France shall know,
And impious deeds shall make her fail and faint.
Then shall thy glory, Jeanne, more splendid grow,
And all pure souls shall then invoke the Saint.

The voices mount towards the skies,
Mingling with angel choirs, whose songs our hopes enhance.
O Jeanne of Arc, now hear our cries!
A second time, a second time, save France!

    1894

HYMN OF JEANNE D'ARC AFTER HER VICTORIES:

All honor and all glory be
To Thee, the Eternal King of kings!
For Thou hast given the victory
To me, a frail and feeble thing.

And thou, dear Mother, pure as snow,
Most lovely star, sublimely bright!
Oh, thou hast been my light below,
Protecting me in danger's night.
Thou, Queen, whose glories ne'er shall fail,
When shall mine eyes thy splendors see?
When shall I rest beneath thy veil,

Never again to part from thee?
Hail, Mary! Holy Mother, hail!

My exiled spirit fain would fly
To heavenly joys that have no end;
Naught here its needs can satisfy,
It craves for God, its perfect Friend.
But, ere that sweet reward begin,
I long to combat for Him here,
For Him unnumbered souls to win,
And find Him dearer and more dear.
My exile here will pass away,
As the day passes and is gone;
Then, up the radiant, sunlit way,
My happy soul shall hasten on,
To see my God in endless day.

PRAYER OF JEANNE D'ARC IN PRISON.

My voices this foretold: I am a prisoner here,
No aid can I expect, except, my God, from Thee;
For love of Thee alone, I left my father dear;
My flower decked fields, blue skies, my flocks, no more I see.
For Thee I left my home and her who gave me birth;
Then, lifting in my hand the standard of Thy choice,
Lord, in Thy holy Name, I led an army forth,
And far famed generals then gave credence to my voice.

Behold my recompense this gloomy prison place,
The price of all my toils, my prayers, my blood, my tears!
No more my flowery fields my longing eyes shall face,
Nor shall I see the home of all my childhood years.
No more shall I behold the mountains far away,
Whose distant summits seemed to pierce the azure sky;
And I shall hear no more the church bells sweetly play.
How soft upon the air those holy notes swept by!

Here, in this gloomy cell, the star I seek in vain,
That used, at vesper hour, to shine so clear and fair;
In vain I seek the leaves, that when upon the plain

Beside my flock I slept, gave cooling shelter there.

Here, when at last I sleep after long bitter weeping,
Of morning's flowers I dream, and perfumes of the dawn;
But then my clanking chains disturb that happy sleeping,-
I wake my dream is past the verdant fields are gone.

Lord, for Thy love I go, martyrdom to embrace;
For Thee I dare to meet the lingering death of fire.
Now but one wish is mine, -to see Thee face to face,
No more to part from Thee: behold my heart's desire!
To die for love of Thee,- what happier lot than this?
I will take up my cross, and walk where Thou hast trod.
Ah! how I long to die, and enter into bliss!
Ah! how I long to die, and thus to see my God!

THE VOICES OF JEANNE D'ARC DURING HER MARTYRDOM:

We have come down from heaven's eternal height,
To smile on thee and bear thee to thy rest.
See in our hands the immortal crown of light,
Designed to grace thy brow, O maiden blest!

Come with us, virgin pure and fair!
Oh! come where saints and martyrs trod;
Come unto joys beyond compare,
Come unto life most fair,
Daughter of God!

Hot burns the fire about thy tender frame,
But far more hotly burns thy holy love;
Soon Christ will call thee to Him by thy name,
And heavenly dews shall soothe thee from above.

An angel comes to set thee free
From every pain; from torture wild.
Behold, the palm descends to thee!
Look up! thy Saviour see,
Great hearted child!

O virgin martyr! one brief moment's pain
Thee shall conduct to heaven beside thy Lord.
Thy death saves France. See! heaven opes again
To her lost children ransomed by thy sword.

JEANE, DYING:

To my eternal home I fly;
Angelic faces meet my view
In God's great Name for France I die!
O Mary, now be nigh!
"Jesu! Jesu!"

THE DIVINE JUDGMENT:

I answer from My throne thy voice that calls My name.
I break thy iron bands, thy bitter foes I shame.
Fly, fly thou pure white dove, to Me, thy Spouse, thy King!
Come, reign with Me in heaven, where Saints thy praise shall sing.

O Jeanne, thy angel brings thee grace;
And I, the Judge of all thy race,
Beside My own throne give thee place,
And this proclaim:
Even in thee I saw love's holy flame.

Thou shalt be crowned. Oh, come to Me!
Thy tears My hand shall wipe away;
My kiss divine I give to thee;
I crown with joy thy griefs to-day.

With thy companions come

To My eternal home;
In heavenly valleys roam,
Following the Lamb.

Soul, well-beloved by Me,
Lo! I have ransomed thee!
Sing the new song, and be

Where'er I am.

Past is thy fleeting shame!
Angels exalt thy name,
Singing thy saintly fame,
Close to My throne.

Ah, timid shepherdess!
Virgin in warrior's dress!
Thy name the world shall bless,
Heavenward blown.
Ah, timid shepherdess!
Virgin in warrior's dress!
All heaven is now thine own.

THE CANTICLE OF TRIUMPH.

THE SAINTS TO JEANNE D'ARC:

The immortal crown to thee, O Jeanne! we bear;
Thou martyr of high God! to thee the palm we bring;
A glorious throne for thee our loving hands prepare,
Beside the King.
Rest now in heaven at last, rest now in heaven, pure bride,
Escaped forevermore from every net and snare!
In endless peace behold! the living waters glide
'Mid fields bestrewn with flowers most fair!
Take thou thy flight; expand thy wings of snow;
For swiftly shalt thou speed from star to golden star.
Through heaven's eternal space, all joyous shalt thou go.
Fly now afar!
No cruel foes are here, no gloomy prison walls;
The shining seraph hosts hail thee their sister blest;
For thee, O spouse of Christ: thy Well Beloved calls.
Find now with Him eternal rest!

JEANNE:

He is my Own. what ecstacy divine!
All heaven is mine own!

THE SAINTS:

All heaven is thine own!

JEANNE:

The angels and the saints, Mary and God, are mine.
They are mine own!

THE SAINTS:

Upon the far off earth ages have passed away,
Since thou didst pass from thence to heaven's eternal joy,
A thousand years in heaven seem but one little day.
O endless day, without alloy!

JEANNE:

O endless day, without or cloud or shade,
No power can snatch from me thy glory all divine!
The passing show of earth from off my sight doth fade,
And heaven is mine!

THE SAINTS:

And heaven is thine!

PRAYER OF FRANCE TO THE VENERABLE JEANNE D'ARC:

In heaven remember, Jeanne, your fatherland,
Remember all her valleys decked with flowers;
Recall the smiling plains, the mountains grand,
You left, to dry her tears, in other hours.
Remember how your arm saved France from deadly foes;
How, like an angel sent from heaven, you cured her woes!
Hear, in her night of pain,
France call on you again:
Remember now!

Remember those great victories you won,
Rheims, Orleans; those memorable days,
When, in God's name, grand deeds by you were done,
Crowning your land with laurels and with bays.
Now, far away from you, I suffer and I sigh.
Come once again to save, who once for me didst die!
Deign now to break my chains,
And all my present pains
Remember now!

My arms with fetters bound, to you I cry,
Dim are my eyes with tears, oh, bring relief!
No longer great among earth's queens am I,
And mine own children pierce my heart with grief.
No more for God they care; their Mother they despise.
O Jeanne, compassionate my myriad miseries!
Daughter of noble heart,
Oh, come, and take my part.
I hope in thee.

CANTICLE TO OBTAIN THE
CANONIZATION OF THE VENERABLE JEANNE D'ARC.

Thy Church, O conquering God! through all the earth,
Begs Thee to crown with the saint's royal crown,
A virgin, martyr, warrior, whose true worth
In heaven's high courts e'en now hath won renown.
Our tumults calm;
Her cause advance!
The halo and the palm
Give unto Jeanne of France!
For guilty France we do not ask from Thee
A mighty conquerer with mail clad horde.
Far better help Jeanne's prayer can gain than he!
One martyr doth outshine all heroes, Lord!

Jeanne is Thy glorious handiwork alone;
A heart of fire, a soldier's soul of steel,
Thou gavest to Thine handmaid, all Thine own,
With lily and laurel crowned, for woe or weal.

Beside her flock she heard the high command, -
Voices from heaven called her to the fray;
So she left all, to save her fatherland;
Conquered by her, the foe fled far away.
To martial hosts she brought God's saving grace;
Her eyes like heaven, her words like burning flame,
Her holiness like theirs who see God's Face.
Bowed sinful souls in penitence and shame.

(O marvel ne'er before in history told!)
A kingdom's crown and glory all undone,
From the strong grasp of the invaders bold,
By a young maiden's feeble arm are won.

Not thy great victories, O Jeanne so blest!
Thy countrymen to celebrate are come;
But thy true glories here they would attest,
Thy purity, thy love, thy martyrdom.

Though she saved France, hers was yet loftier grace,
The gift Christ gave to those who loved Him best,
Beside His cross to have the nearest place,
He gave to Jeanne, before He gave her rest.

In that last torture of consuming fire
She heard her "voices" speak once more her name,
And left earth's exile for her heart's desire,
Angel of France! up that steep path of flame.

Daughter of God! deign now our voice to hear!
Descend to us with thy sweet heavenly glance!
Come, and convert the land to thee so dear!
A second time, a second time, save France!

By God's great power
In thee displayed,
Save France! O come, save France,
Thou saintly warrior maid!

Glorious' O thou strong child of God! wast thou,
When English hosts to meet thee did not dare;
Yet, in thy father's fields,- remember now,-
Once weak and tender lambs were in thy care.

Of all the weak
Be the defence!
In hearts of children meek,
Preserve their innocence!

Sweet martyr! keep our convents in thy care!
Our virgins are thy sisters, each thine own,
And like to thine the object of their prayer,--
To see God reign in every heart alone.

This their desire,
All souls to save.
Now let them share thy fire,
Apostle, martyr brave!

When holy Church shall give thee crown and palm,
How swiftly every fear in us will faint!
Then can we sing in loud afid rapturous psalm,
To Jeanne, our virgin, martyr, warrior, saint,-

God grants us hope
Through thee today
Saint Jeanne, Saint Jeanne of
France, Pray for thy
country, pray!

    1894.

* Sister Teresa's full name in religion was Sister Teresa of the Child Jesus and the Holy Face

Printed in Great Britain
by Amazon